CareerBall

Sun Devil Athletics Student-Athlete Career Guide and Handbook

CHRIS SMITH
Chief Executive Officer
Career Athletes
and
RUSS HAFFERKAMP
Author of
CareerBall
The Sport Athletes Play When They're Through Playing Sports

Sun Devil Athletics
Student-Athlete Career Guide and Handbook

Arizona State University
Sun Devil Athletics

Student-Athlete Development
Sun Devil Life Skills Program

ISBN-13: 978-1484809983
ISBN-10: 148480998X

Copyright: 2010 by CareerBall™. All rights reserved. Printed in the United States of America. No part of this book may be used or reproduced in any manner whatsoever without written permission of the author. Other than the custom message appearing on page iii, the author, and no other party, organization or individual, is responsible for creating the content within this book.

Warning/Liability/Warranty: The author and publisher have made every attempt to provide the reader with accurate, timely, and useful information. However, given the rapid changes taking place in today's economy and job market, some of our information will inevitably change. The information presented here is for reference purposes only. The author and publisher make no claim that using this information will guarantee the reader a job. The author and publisher shall not be liable for any losses or damages incurred in the process of following the advice of this book.

About Russ Hafferkamp: Russ Hafferkamp is a former NCAA All-American, CEO of the Athlete Career Network, Inc. and Managing Director of Career Athletes, LLC. Russ is recognized as a leader and coach in the career planning of high school, collegiate and elite athletes and author of *'CareerBall: The Sport Athletes Play When They're Through Playing Sports'*. Additional information can be found on page 171 or at **www.careerball.net**.

About CareerBall™: *'CareerBall: The Sport Athletes Play When They're Through Playing Sports'* is the #1 career guide that coaches the competitive athlete through all the steps necessary to achieve a competitive edge in today's job market. Read the reviews or available for sale at **www.careerball.net**. Get updates and regular go-to advice by visiting the Athlete Career Blog at **www.careerball.net/blog**.

> **About Career Athletes:** Founded in 1998, Career Athletes (www.CareerAthletes.com) is the premier destination for hundreds of thousands current & alumni student-athletes who seek to create and share outstanding professional networking relationships and career education/job opportunities. Its mission is to assist competitive athletes, athletic departments and employers by providing a wide range of helpful career training and communication tools, including access to a secure, compliant network of customized, interactive communities for each individual athletic department. Career Athletes is owned and managed by former student-athletes with offices in Kansas, Washington, Georgia, Florida, New Jersey and California.

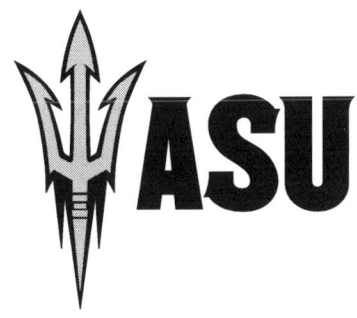

Message from Senior Associate Athletic Director Jean Boyd

At Arizona State University, over 500 young men and women on 21 teams actively represent Sun Devil Athletics and compete for conference and national championships each year. Simultaneously, as one of these young men or women you have been embedded in a university experience that is Top 100 in the world! Since your arrival at Arizona State, you have lived The Sun Devil Way. We appreciate the energy, passion, and commitment that you have poured into being a Sun Devil student-athlete.

As the student-athlete chapter of your life comes to a close, you will transition from the structured life of college and competitive athletics to opportunities and careers that will fulfill your life's potential. For many, this transitional period will be navigated gracefully while for others it may be a confusing and frustrating experience. As a Sun Devil Student-Athlete you learned to **Compete with Passion and Character** in all that you do. The Sun Devil Life Skills Program was designed to prepare student-athletes for a competitive job market and we have provided you with information and skills to navigate the next step in life's journey. Be confident and **RELENTLESS** in your approach and use the knowledge you have gained!

We are pleased to provide to you "CareerBall", our Sun Devil Athletics Student-Athlete Career Guide and Handbook, as a resource that offers information about "going pro" in life. All of Sun Devil Athletics is committed to helping you achieve great success. While your time as a student-athlete is coming to an end, you are a **Sun Devil for LIFE!** Do not hesitate to call on us as a resource as you transition to a Championship Life.

Go Devils!

Jean Boyd
Senior Associate Athletic Director

Table of Contents

Introduction ix

Chapter 1

This is Your Wake-Up Call

Let's Put Your Career Transition into Perspective 1
Welcome to the Rest of Your Life 2
It's Time to Plan Ahead 3
You're Already Prepared For Your First Career 4
Finding the Right Fit 5
Heads-up!... Two Important Points to Remember 6
Let's Play a Little Game Called 'CareerBall' 7

Chapter 2

Understanding Your Athlete DNA

One of a Kind... for Better or Worse 9
Athletics Largely Shape Who We Are 10
Unique Opportunities For Collegiate Athletes 11
Unique Challenges Facing Collegiate Athletes 12
It's a Scientific Fact: Career Development for Athletes is Difficult 13
Athletes are at Risk for 'Stereotype Threat' 14
Student-Athletes Face a Tough Task: 'Role Strain' 15
Balancing Academics vs. Athletics: Part 1 17
Balancing Academics vs. Athletics: Part 2 18
The Choices You Make Stay With You a Lifetime 19
Are You a "Tunnel Vision" Athlete? 20
Dumb Jock or Scholar-Athlete?... Your Choice 21
One Bad Apple Spoils the Whole Bunch 22
The Trend is Improving 23
The 'Dark Side' of Highly Competitive Athletes 24
Are You an "Alpha Personality?" 24
What About Alpha Females? 25
If You Think You Might Be an Alpha Athlete... 26
Do You Need Help? 28

Chapter 3

Why Athletes Make Great Employees!

Interpreting and Leveraging Your Athlete "Soft Skills" 31
What Can Athlete DNA Do in the Workforce? 32
Common Traits Within the Athlete DNA 34
Valuable Currency that Counts 37
10 Primary Traits Why Athletes Are Successful in the Workplace 38
There Are Also 16 Secondary Traits for Your Success 40
Employers Define "Intelligence" in Many Ways 41

Chapter 4

Real World Strategies for College Athletes

- Start Planning for Your Future Career Today 43
- Selecting a Major... and a Career 43
- A Typical College "Career Prep" Schedule 45
- Make Time for Some Experience 47
- The #1 Most Valuable Activity You Can Do! 49
- How Do You Prepare for Informational Interviews? 51
- Take Responsibility for Your Career! 51
- Professional Athletes: Special Issues and Considerations 53

Chapter 5

Assessing Your Personal Interests

- Finding the Right Fit 57
- First Up: Assess Yourself 58
- Do Personality Tests Work? 59
- Indentifying Your Work Personality is Important 60
- Ranking Your Work Values 61
- Matching Your Work Interests 64
- Job Satisfaction is Very Important 66
- What is Your Individual Athlete Trait Profile? 67
- Your Individual Athlete Core Message 69

Chapter 6

The Power of the Mentor

- Characteristics of a Good Mentor 72
- The Right Mentor Can Help Develop Your Career 73
- Make Your Relationship with Your Mentor Meaningful 73
- Questions to Ask Your Mentor 75
- How to Repay Your Mentor 78

Chapter 7

Creating A Network That Works

- Utilizing the Good Ol' Boy Network... Especially if You're a Woman 79
- The Power of Common Interests and Information 80
- Building Your Network 81
- Prepare to Work at Networking 83
- Do's & Don'ts of Networking 84

Chapter 8

Winning Resumes and Cover Letters

- Your Resume is Your Calling Card 87
- Key Resume Rules 88
- Visual Appearance of Your Resume 89
- The Best Resume Format 90
- Sample Athlete Resume Format 91

Keywords and Scanned Resumes 92
What You Should Never Include in Your Resume: 93
Overcoming No Previous Experience or a Low GPA 93
Cover Letters Count...Probably More Than You Think 94
What About References? Do I Really Need Them? 96
Try These Extra Tricks 97

Chapter 9

Job Interviews and What's Important

Still the Most Important Hiring Criteria 99
Employers Hire People for Their Future, Rather Than Their Past 100
Preparation is the Key 101
Interview Etiquette 103
The Application Process 105
The Main Event – The Interview 106
Frequently Asked Questions (FAQs) 109
Here are Some Common Interview Questions 110
What About Illegal Questions? 115
Ask Your Own Questions 116
Remember These Do's and Don'ts 117
Interview Follow-Up 120
References 120

Chapter 10

Overcoming Life's Little Screw-ups

Arrest Records, Poor Credit, Lousy GPA? Ouch! 123
Background Checks 124
What Can You Do to Prepare? 126
Bad Credit = Bad Apple 127
Drinking and Driving (DUI) 128
Misdemeanors 128
Overcoming a Serious Criminal Conviction 130

Chapter 11

Tips from the Pros

Career Pointers From Former Collegiate Athletes 135
What Advice Would You Give A Current College Athlete? 136
What Real World Advice Do You Have On Finding A Career? 139
What Specific Skills Did You Acquire As A Competitive Athlete
That Helps You In Your Career? 142

Chapter 12

Think Big... but Think Smart

Most of Us Will Not be Bill Gates or LeBron James 145
Everything is Changing 146
Be Smart About Your Athletic Career 147
Be Smart About Your Education 148

Be Smart About Getting a Variety of Experience	148
Be Smart in Your Job Search	149
Be Smart About Money	151
Be Smart About Your Credit History	152
Be Smart About Lifelong Learning	152
Be Smart About "Plan B"	153
Graduate School? A Pretty Good Option	154
Be Smart About Your Generation	156

Chapter 13

Current Employment Trends Shaping the New Economy

Career Trends to Watch in The New Economy	160
14 Emerging Trends You Should Also Keep Your Eye On	163
Business-as-Usual is a Thing of the Past	167
Don't Lose Hope... Ever!	168

Chapter 14

Need More Help?

Make an Appointment With the Career Center!	169
Here is a list of the some of the services you can access at the Career Center:	169
Register with CareerAthletes.com	170

About the Author

Russ Hafferkamp	171

Introduction

One of my favorite sayings is *'instant gratification takes too long'*. But there is no escaping the fact that every competitive athlete will have to commit nearly the same amount of time, energy, and self-responsibility that they applied to sports if they want to be successful in their career.

At any given time, over 400,000 young men and women actively participate in collegiate athletics, or at the elite international or professional level in the United States. Millions more are active in high school sports. Each of these athletes will ultimately make the transition from the structured life of high school, college, and competitive athletics to jobs and careers that will fulfill their life's potential. For many, this transitional period will be navigated gracefully and without incident; for many others it will be a confusing and frustrating experience.

CareerBall is what you learn to play after you've mastered competitive baseball, football, or basketball (or any organized sport), but before you get to play the game called *PayCheckBall*– the game that pays the bills, fuels the car, stocks the refrigerator, and lets you move out of your parents' house. *CareerBall* is a good game to learn… It's fun, exciting, fast-paced, high-scoring, competitive… and the best part is that you're never too young to learn it!

The good news/bad news part of reading *CareerBall* is pretty simple: Thus far, being a competitive athlete most of your life has provided you with a slew of valuable "soft skills" that are easily transferred to the workplace, and you're about to learn what it takes to make the most of this transition. But, sadly, being a highly competitive athlete has also left you somewhat unprepared, or "behind-the-curve" in your job search and career prep skills.

> *To help you get started, the contents of CareerBall are presented in a 'keep it simple' format. It's part lecture, part how-to manual, and with many different chapters to allow you to cherry-pick the knowledge within depending upon where you are in your own career development. Inside each chapter resides some of the most important tried-and-true, up-to-date gems of career advice that you can use to insure a happy path when you have concluded full-time athletics. Also, keep an eye out for the information contained inside these shadow boxes ... it will be thought-provoking and highlight important points in each chapter.*

I hope you enjoy the game of *CareerBall*... the sport *every* athlete plays when they're through playing sports!

Chapter 1

This is Your Wake-Up Call

"It's tough to climb the ladder of success, especially if you're trying to keep your nose to the grindstone, your shoulder to the wheel, your eye on the ball, and your ear to the ground."

Let's Put Your Career Transition into Perspective

There are generally two distinct camps that competitive athletes fall into when the subject of career planning is raised:

1. Those that screw up, screw around, or just don't care enough and eventually "evolve" into their careers, and

2. Those that "get it" early on in the process, identify their talents, and point themselves in the right direction.

By far, the biggest challenge you will face as a competitive athlete is determining which camp you are in.

> *Although there will be many transitions in your life, few have the potential to be as important or challenging as ending your competitive playing career. At some point, every student-athlete ends his or her competitive career. For many, this event will coincide with the completion of their athletic eligibility– what might be called a planned or expected transition. For others, though, termination of their sports careers may be unexpected, caused by things like career-ending injuries or being cut from the team or a simple loss of interest in the chase.*

Chances are also good that, if you're reading this book, you're either:

1. *Not Very Interested* in your own career development after you finish up a lifetime of competitive athletics, and your mind only occasionally asks "What's next?", or

2. *Very Interested* in your career development now because sports is all you've known, and that life appears to be ending (like it or not), or

3. ***Absolutely Freaking Out!...*** You're finished, or almost finished with collegiate sports and are wondering what are the best steps to take toward getting a job and pursuing a meaningful career development plan, because you have got to pull it together and get on with the rest of your life.

Well, not to worry… you're not alone! Over 400,000 competitive athletes around the country are currently wrapped up, or are heads-down, in sports and are on the same path as you. The good news is that what you will read in *CareerBall* will help you identify the most important steps you can take in establishing a self-identity that is less "talented athlete"… and more "talented employee" or "talented entrepreneur," a valuable commodity in today's working world.

> *As you make your way through this guide, you'll begin to realize that the toughest part of the transition that men and women competitive athletes must make from a lifetime of sports to the working world does not come as easily as hitting a ball, running a play, or achieving your best time. As an athlete, this difficult transition can be the biggest emotional and psychological challenge that you will face in your lifetime– one for which you might oftentimes be unprepared, and one in which there is little wise advice and counsel from that ever-present "coach" you've had by your side since the Pee Wee leagues.*

A big part of the athlete transition issue is centered on a "tunnel vision syndrome" that affects all highly competitive athletes to varying degrees at some stage of their lives. Parents can usually see it, high school coaches and college athletic administrators can see it, professional sports agents and general managers see it… and, yes, hiring managers see it at companies large and small all across America. Unfortunately, athletes who are unaware that they suffer from tunnel vision spend way too much time thinking only about sports (training, competition, etc.) and, as a result, a large number of athletes are left ill-prepared for the balanced perspective required of "real world" career opportunities. Some call this behavior crazy or blind, some call it self-centered, and some call it selfish. In the simplest terms, it's called "tunnel vision." But no matter what you call it, the effect of this kind of one-track thinking is the same… and each and every athlete needs to be aware of the 'opportunity costs' of such an affliction.

Welcome to the Rest of Your Life

Maybe you heard it mentioned at your graduation ceremony in high school… maybe your parents uttered the words… maybe you've never heard them before… but, sooner or later, when the reality sinks in, these words, when strung together, have a frightening message:

"Welcome to the rest of your life…"

… and welcome, I might add, to one of the most critical challenges facing most competitive athletes.

It's a known fact that many competitive athletes are not well prepared for the transitional challenges that face them as they move from playing on a team to the highly competitive work world. But I have worked with thousands of competitive athletes over the years, and the one thing that stands out in almost every athlete I've met is that athletes, in general, are very talented men and women capable of achieving any goal they set their mind towards.

While it sounds scary, the transition to the work world after an exciting career of competitive athletics should (and will) be one of the most enjoyable periods in your life. Most importantly of all, most of you will find jobs and enjoy plentiful careers that build on your positive attitudes, strengths, and values and utilize many of the skills that helped form you into a successful athlete in the first place.

Whether or not your transition from athlete-to-career will be stressful will depend on a couple of important factors:

> First, how do you perceive the transition? For example, do you see this termination as a beginning with exciting new challenges and opportunities to be enjoyed, or do you view it in your sports career as a significant loss, leaving you devastated, disoriented, and without direction or meaning in your life?

> Second, what is your identification with the athlete role? Student-athletes who identify strongly with multiple roles (such as those of athlete, student, family member, and significant other) are more likely to cope effectively with the transition than those who see themselves solely as an athlete.

Although you may not be close to the end of your college athletic career, it is never too soon to begin planning for your transition out of sports. It's the really smart athletes that begin thinking now about what you want to do after your sports career has ended, and then take action to move towards that goal.

It's Time to Plan Ahead

Try as we may to control our destiny, life is often tough, unpredictable, and serendipitous. What, for example, will your work life be like in another twelve or twenty-four months... or even five years from now? The old days when you can expect to work for one company most of your life have nearly vanished. Most people in today's job market can realistically expect to undergo three to five career changes and hold more than fifteen different jobs during their lifetime. Long-term loyalty to a single employer is no longer expected, since many people change jobs and employers within a few years.

Athletes are accustomed to performing well. Sometimes they carry the standard of excellence with them into career exploration. Athletes may look at only jobs that they are familiar with or are confident about, usually careers in athletics. They're confident in their ability to coach, for example, but less sure about careers in which they have no experience. It's easy to forget that developing a career is really just like beginning a new sport; it requires practice, and the new steps may feel awkward at first.

Your goal is to find a job based on your strengths rather than your needs. Searching for a job is never fun, and if you're fortunate, you'll never have to search for many jobs in your life. But if you're not experienced at looking for work or even thinking about work, the planning and search process can be arduous at best.

Many competitive athletes make job or career transitions by accident. They do little other than take advantage of opportunities that may arise unexpectedly. If you truly believe you can find a job simply by leveraging your athletic experience and contacts, please think again... this is a myth, my friend!

> *We live in a post-industrial, high-tech society which requires employees to demonstrate both intelligence and concrete work skills– not just athletic accomplishments or a recommendation from important alumni. Lacking the necessary skills and mobility required for getting jobs in such high-tech, growth-oriented communities will be tough obstacles to overcome if all you have to show on your resume is a long history of touchdowns and team spirit.*

Ultimately, you, like all student-athletes, will reach the point where your competitive collegiate career will draw to an end. Some will be ready for this transition, and others will not. If you want to be one of those who is on a happy path, plan in advance to make this transition a positive one. Retirement from a full-time commitment for athletics does not have to be a depressing event. But it is important to acknowledge the occasional and growing unhappy path of athletes ending their sports careers, where depression is becoming more widespread because people have not developed additional outlets of expression and performance that they can continue throughout their lives. If you only participated in sports, you may be suffering from tunnel vision, and you simply must remember and constantly tell yourself that sports are really only a temporary obsession in the big-world picture.

Finally, if your transition from sports is overly stressful, expected or unexpected, make sure you seek assistance so you can better cope with the inevitable. You may have access to many terrific resources within your athletic department and on campus, or confide in your parents, talk to your coach, or we'll help you get a career coach. If all else fails in your immediate support group, shoot me a note (russ@careerball.net), and I'll try to help you navigate the maze. With a little effort and some positive reinforcement, we'll get you in the right frame of mind.

You're Already Prepared For Your First Career

In many ways, sports has been your first career. Some people have been lucky enough to just fall into the perfect job right as they finish their last minute of eligibility or leave their sport "for good." But finding the right career need not depend solely on luck. Actively searching for the right career (often called a career plan) does require a great deal of preparation, planning, determination, and some luck. Career development is the processes of making good transition decisions in order to facilitate your dreams of a successful and rewarding career.

The good news is your participation in sports has not been a waste of time. For while you have been competing in athletics for most of your life, you've acquired many important skills and values that will serve you well in the future. It will serve you well to remember, though, that sports can be a dual-edged sword.

> On one side, sport can provide you with numerous opportunities to learn about yourself and others.

> On the other side, an exclusive commitment to sport can dominate your life so much that you won't be prepared for any other activity.

You need to devote enormous amounts of time and energy to perfecting your athletic skills. If these efforts come at the expense of education or your preparation for other life activities, you may have nothing to turn to when you're sport career ends.

Who has time to prepare and set up for a career after sports? The answer, sadly, is that most competitive athletes do not have the time to adequately prepare for their future after sports and are sacrificing greatly without even knowing it.

> *On the other hand, your athletic involvement gives you many advantages that students who are non-athletes will never experience. But are you actually willing to sacrifice your future earning potential for a limited sports involvement after high school? Hopefully, I'm not the first person to say this to you but, "Hey... wake up, sports fans... how about a little balance here? A hundred% of mindless dedication to anything– sports included– is a ridiculous and dangerous path to be on, and you need to snap out of it... PRONTO!"*

Finding the Right Fit

In your sport, it is important to find a position that best suits your talents. In your career, it is no different; you want to find the occupation and work setting that best fits your personality and athlete DNA so you can maximize your chances of career success and satisfaction.

The better the fit, the more satisfied you will be, and the longer and better you are likely to work in your chosen career. A poor fit creates unhappy workers and employers. The best way to optimize the fit is to identify and articulate what you do well. Be sure you communicate your transferable skills and abilities, what you like to do (your interests), what is important to you (your values), and how you typically interact with others and with the environment (personality style).

People who are highly successful and also love their work year after year spend most of their time at work engaged in activities that make use of their strongest abilities and match their personalities. They spend very little time performing functions for which they have no special gift or interest. Their lives are concentrating on doing what they do best. The people that you know who are both successful and happy with their work have found their natural self-expression; their talents and personalities are perfectly lined with what they do.

Heads-up!... Two Important Points to Remember

For over 30 years, I have advised thousands of highly competitive athletes on how to prepare for the proverbial 'life after sports'… and help them make the most of their career choices and opportunities. The main core of my advice centers around two central themes:

> ➤ First, you must thoroughly understand the vast array of "transferable skills" acquired through athletic experiences and how to leverage them in your job search and career, and,

> ➤ Second, you must thoroughly understand, and commit to a list of fundamental disciplines about self-assessment, going about your job search and career growth in the correct (and intelligent) fashion, and seeking out and learning from others who have successfully traversed the road before you.

But, today, there are two important cultural points that need to be recognized by athletes who are thinking about their career development after a lifetime of sports.

1. Times Have Changed

Generally speaking, most athletes that are actively participating in sports today have grown-up in a society that has provided vast amounts of entitlement and instant gratification. "What's in it for me?" was an attitude held by many athletes. With the recent changes in our economic and political climate, society today holds a very different view towards athlete entitlement. But while times have changed, the athletes who have been conditioned to operate within an athlete-centric culture, continue to be caught up in believing that a 100% commitment to organized sports will always produce a great outcome in life… and in our careers. But sadly, unless you're making seven figures a year and signed to a multi-year deal, being a good athlete is no guarantee that you will succeed in your career after sports… or even find a job, for that matter.

> *It's also important to realize that we are now living in times where most of the rules have changed… especially when it comes to the timing of making important life decisions and nurturing a meaningful career. In the not-so-distant past, career planning and career development was rewarded mostly by just showing up to the interview. Today, though, career planning and development requires more preparation and effort, and a little luck. The bottom line is, today, if you want to achieve success in your career, the fundamentals are still the same as they were yesterday but you must begin to think about your career much earlier in life and remember that preparation and effort are key.*

2. You're on Your Own Now

To be fair, we athletes have had it pretty easy... with a lot of help along the way. Our parents (who supported our initial efforts by making sure we were enrolled in sports) made the try-outs, drove us everywhere, fought the politics of all-star teams, and were always emotionally invested in our early success, even if they didn't make all our games all the time.

Our coaches have also been there along every step of the way, whether it was our club coach, high school coach, or even our uncles, grandmother, or skill coaches– whomever looked after us as we participated in our sports career along the way. College, nowadays, is also very much invested in our sports: special recruitment packages, pre-enrollment, class tutors, life-skills training... you name it, colleges today provide most every athlete with some type of assistance.

But then, reality sets in. Sports are over, and all the coaches, agents, administrators, handlers, and, sadly, even some parents, vanish... leaving you with a depressing feeling of starting over. And this time when you glance behind you to check on your entourage, you may realize you're on your own!

Let's Play a Little Game Called 'CareerBall'

The time has come whereby everybody associated with competitive athletics– college administrators, coaches, parents... even YOU!– need to wake up, step up, and commit to your career in ways you may have never thought of or have been told about. And the earlier you do this in your athletic life, the better.

Are you ready?.... Let's play *CareerBall*. Remember, though... just like real sports, this game will produce winners and losers. But we're fairly certain that if you put in those two timeless qualities we spoke about earlier– preparation and effort– you will score nicely and ultimately win in this game of life. Good Luck.

> *One final note: This game called 'CareerBall' is not a game that will make everyone feel optimistic about leaving the safe and predictable confines of organized sports– that world we live in where excitement, recognition, status, and perks have become the norm. At sometime or another, almost every athlete will have to say "Good-bye" to the fabulous, intoxicating environment of full-time competitive athletics. And when that time comes, a rewarding (and at times terrifying) new world order will open up for you. While we're probably not the first to say "Welcome to the real world", we are pretty certain we're the first to say "Welcome to CareerBall".*

Chapter 2

Understanding Your Athlete DNA

One of a Kind... for Better or Worse

DNA is often compared to a set of blueprints, a recipe, or a code since it contains the instructions needed to construct who you are. To become a highly competitive athlete, it's safe to say you have terrific physical DNA that equips you with attributes like speed, quickness, intelligence, strength, etc. But what about your mental DNA... the stuff inside your head that makes you coachable, competitive, accountable, and a natural leader? Believe it or not, understanding what's made you successful on the field will help you become successful in your career.

When people become highly skilled at anything they were not forced to learn, they are probably expressing a natural gift. One person might learn multiple languages with incredible ease, while another person has very little ability to learn languages but possesses a gift for downhill skiing. Someone born with a collection of innate abilities has an easier time learning certain things, and they turn each progressive skill corner much more easily.

Each of us has already been dealt a very specific hand of cards by our genetic inheritance of talent and ability. That gives us a knack for playing a great game of lacrosse, tennis, or water polo... and, going forward in life, a fairly narrow range of roles in the working world that we can enjoy with natural ease and mastery.

But just as our DNA makes each of us a one-of-a-kind individual with abilities to do certain kinds of things easily and happily, that same DNA and can make other tasks seem like pure torture. Aptitudes you were born with are completely different from acquired knowledge, skills, and interest. Over your lifetime, your interests can change. You can gain new skills and knowledge. But your natural, inherent talents remain with you for your entire life; and for the most part, Mother Nature, doesn't let you change them except to improve upon them.

> *As with sports, the better you understand your unique genetic gifts, the more likely you can choose a satisfying and successful career. People are happiest when they combine their strongest abilities in a career that makes full use of all or most of them. The further people stray from using their natural gifts, the greater the chance they will be dissatisfied with their careers.*

This dissatisfaction can show up in two ways: boredom and burnout. Boredom frequently signals that your abilities are not being fully expressed. On the other hand, if certain parts of the job remain difficult or unpleasant no matter how many times you do them, you may not have the a natural gift in that department and simply tire of the routine. Therefore, it's possible to be bored and burned out at the same time. I know of many athletes who get burned out and were bored... and they stopped playing. But I know many more people who are burned out and bored at work and still can't quit their jobs.

Athletics Largely Shape Who We Are

The licensed establishment known as organized athletics serves us well in two important areas:

1. It is a great training ground to find out who you are, what you are made of, and what you're capable of doing.

2. It provides you with exposure to an environment from which to learn the human interaction skills necessary to be confident and successful in your life.

Organized sports, particularly in high school and at the major college level, are also an exercise in submission to social control. Within this environment, rules, conformity, plays, media, expectation, measurement, referees and pressure all conspire to make you an integral part of the team, like it or not.

By contrast, unorganized sports like pick-up ball, four-square, hopscotch, or the other playground sports we all grew up on, provided our most important life lessons. First and foremost, unorganized sports taught us a great deal about collective governance and constant conflict resolution. Pick-up ball harks back to a traditional time when kids weren't scheduled into play dates or stashed with adult supervision, but instead made their way to the park on their own, picked teams, had fun, and sorted it all out... conflicts, disagreements, start and stop times, rules, team selections, and who was out and who was safe. It was on the playground where most athletes molded their athlete DNA and grew up along the way.

Pick-up sports are where you first learn about heart and fairness and all the ethical elements learned within sports that serve athletes well in their post-sports work career. Most games, from one-on-one basketball to ultimate Frisbee, have to be fairly played, or the whole system breaks down and everyone's fun is compromised. As an athlete, you practice an honor code, making your own calls and giving them up. You learn what character is, and who has it or who doesn't. In pick-up sports, you learn to quickly reach judgments about temperament and collaborative aptitude. Over time, there's the emotional containment that you learn to bring to the court, even if only to ensure that no one sees or hears the emotions you don't want them to see or hear.

> *Somewhere along the way while playing sports, you learn to have fun– but you also learn how to be tough and intensely competitive. It's not an easy balancing act to try to get along with everyone as you try to find a way to win. And, you learn about being a part of something and finishing it up. You learn about discipline, handling disappointments, being more team-oriented, and realizing that not everything is about you. You could score, but could you pass?*

On the turf field, on the court, in the pool, or on the track, every athlete gets a lesson in community organization and education. It is where you can make your closest friends, whether they were from a different neighborhood, on a different team, or of a different color. It is an environment where your GPA, your religion, or your sex couldn't be a disadvantage. The respect you received playing sports was usually a direct result of the respect you gave.

Unique Opportunities For Collegiate Athletes

As a student-athlete, a big reason you went to college, if not the primary reason, was to compete in your sport. Sure, you would have probably gone to college if you were not an athlete, however, sports certainly played an important role in you making the jump from high school to college. Regardless of the reason of how you got into college, it's the successful transition out of college that has our attention now, and this transition may be more difficult than you think.

Although a primary focus for many student-athletes is their sports, the real value of college extends far beyond the playing field. College presents the opportunity to learn and think and to critically evaluate information; it exposes you to people with different backgrounds, values, and worldviews, and it introduces you to new ideas. For others, though, the value of pursuing a college degree is more practical: a university education is an investment in future earning potential.

While you're in college, it's rare to realize just how special your experience is and understand how so few people ever get to experience anything close to being a college athlete. And if you're in college, you're in the right place. As more and more businesses require higher levels of education and training, a college degree is becoming a passport to the upper levels of the world of work.

For some student-athletes, a university is nothing more than a training ground for a future career in professional sports. For others, it is an opportunity to pursue an education– an opportunity they might not have received if it were not for athletics. Everyone has the choice as to how you experience your time spent in college, but the fundamental question remains: Do you want college to be a place where you find personal, athletic, educational, cultural, and intellectual growth and excellence– or do you simply want to be a place where you put some time before you move on to the next phase of your life?

> *For the vast majority of college athletes, graduation means the end of their formal sports career. Only a few go on to careers in professional sports, and by-and-large, a professional sports career does not realistically exist for the vast majority of student-athletes, either because of a lack the ability at the next level or because their sport does not offer great professional opportunities. In either case, you can make an easier transition out of formal sports participation by preparing in advance for life after college.*

Unique Challenges Facing Collegiate Athletes

For collegiate student-athletes who have spent a large portion of their lives striving and competing to conquer their respective athletic skills, many find their identities have been formed in association to their sports. So what happens when their careers are over? For the few elite student-athletes who won't be affected by the ceiling of NCAA eligibility, there is an option of continuing on to a professional level, but for the large majority, their days of practice will soon be a routine of the past. This concept of retirement is an issue that runs deeper than just loss-of-sport. It is often a difficult transition affecting student-athletes in many spheres of their lives. Athletes transitioning from full-time college sports participation to the working world may experience many different types of loss, such as:

A loss of belonging

It is not uncommon for student-athletes to experience sadness of the loss-of-sport or fear of an unknown future because of the change in time demands and sadness over the loss of belonging to the team. You go from twenty to thirty hours a week of practice and competition to having nothing to do. As a result, you are forced to form a new identity. You go from being "Tim the hockey player," to a working person sometimes in a huge city where thousands of people do the exact same thing that you do. This emotional leap is quite hard, and it's natural to feel loneliness. After all, for four years you see the same people every day, and all of a sudden, it is gone. In a sense, you begin to feel out of touch.

A loss of purpose

Athletes often feel a loss of purpose and find it hard to get the same satisfaction out of their new endeavors as opposed to athletic competition. When you are on the team, you feel like you are striving toward something, and you feel great when you master your personal and team goals. Let's face it: most work doesn't make much of a difference, and it's difficult to get the same satisfaction out of a hard day of work as you did out of a hard practice.

A loss of competition

> *One of the hardest things for athletes to overcome is the loss of competition. Aside from sports and office politics, where else are you going to find the challenge of playing week-in and week-out in a competitive league? Today's world is less about straight-up competition and more about working together, and highly competitive athletes are junkies for competition, which is the very essence of sports.*

Most sports psychologists agree that retirement will be more difficult for students with a strong identity as an athlete. Students who have been playing their sports from a very young age and who have made few friends outside of their sport will probably struggle more than the students who spent more time developing other parts of him or herself.

An athlete's negligence of other areas of their lives is often reinforced by coaches, family members, and friends who are more interested in the athlete's success than his or her personal growth. Consequently, those who neglect other aspects of personal interest risk feeling ignored, used, and forgotten at the termination of their careers.

For some athletes, though, the end of a college career isn't all negative. Many are ready to move on with their lives and take on new opportunities. The demanding lifestyle of a college athlete can be very stressful, and athletes can often feel a sense of relief and anticipation when their playing days are complete. It's not uncommon to hear, "I loved my experience, but I couldn't do it for four more years." To these athletes, the future is their new playing field where they can begin (many of them for the first time) to be identified as a person rather than just an athlete.

It's a Scientific Fact: Career Development for Athletes is Difficult

You should know a few things about being a collegiate athlete that were not advertised in advance and are a downside of being an athlete in college.

First, researchers in sport psychology (the people who spend their lives studying these types of things), have conducted studies that support the notion that college athletes often compare unfavorably to non-athletes in terms of issues related to vocational and career development. Non-athletes have been found to score higher than athletes on measures of career maturity, vocational maturity, and the formulation of mature educational and career plans. These studies seem to indicate that college athletes experience less career development and maturity than non-athletes. Ouch!

These sports researchers also go on to introduce plausible reasoning why athletes compare unfavorably to non-athletes in early career development. One of the related factors that might influence an athlete's level of career development is "athletic community," which is defined as "the degree to which an individual identifies with the athlete role." It appears that individuals who have a strong athletic identity place great importance on being involved in sport, which may actually hinder career development among athletes. More specifically, sports psychologists have hypothesized that athletes with a high athletic identity may engage in fewer exploratory behaviors, experience "identity foreclosure," and perceive their "life role" as solely that of an athlete, which may inadvertently postpone career decisions.

> *Another plausible sports-related theory is that an early life focus on athletics is also a significant factor that inhibits career development. Athletes often develop a strong commitment to sports early in life through reinforcement from parents, coaches, and peers. Although a strong commitment to sports is certainly a desirable characteristic from an athletic point of view, many leading psychologists have theorized that such a strong commitment may be harmful in areas outside of sports, including career development.*

What we do know as the truth today is that college athletes lag behind their non-athlete peers in formulating career goals and plans. College athletes generally have more time constraints placed on them than non-athletes; for example, practice, training room time, road trips, film, study hall, nutrition, etc. Further, the life of a college athlete is often highly structured, with many important decisions made by others (e.g., coaches, academic coordinators, and team cultures). Taken together, these factors may cause the college athlete to feel that he or she is lacking in terms of tangible, practical, occupational information. Throw in the fact that most athletes never make professional ranks, and often a college sports commitment simply does not prepare an athlete for a career outside of athletics.

Here's what all this means: While it may receive passing attention and action by a few, it is becoming readily apparent to parents, coaches, athletic administrators, agents, and self-aware athletes that the growing importance of a young athlete being prepared for life outside of the sporting role is a real-life issue– an issue that must be radically addressed so that successful athletes do not begin their real life at a serious disadvantage.

Athletes are at Risk for 'Stereotype Threat'

A few years ago, a major study of seventy-one Division III member institutions of the NCAA documented a significant academic achievement gap separating male athletes and non-athletes at selective liberal arts colleges. Although admissions practices (potentially biased in favor of enrolling athletes) might be to blame for this gap, studies also suggest that the perceived threat among athletes of confirming the negative stereotype of the dumb jock might also help perpetuate the gap.

Stereotype threat refers to 'the perceived risk of confirming, through one's behavior or outcomes, negative stereotypes that are held about one's social identity'. As a result, the stigma attached to athletic participation at some selective institutions might trigger this stereotype threat response among athletes, accounting for some portion of their weaker academic performance.

Did you ever hear the expression "When everyone tells you that you are sick, you tend to lie down"? It's the same for stereotypes such as "dumb jock." No one really thinks the athletically-inclined are born less intelligent than the rest of world, but as athletes, they tend to get away with less studying and are expected to take less challenging classes. A college football or basketball player simply doesn't have the time between practice and away games, publicity, and so forth to study as hard to those who have a lot less on their proverbial plates. And, if you call someone "dumb" and that's all you expect from them, and you do it long enough, she or he will definitely slump to your expectations.

This term "stereotype threat" was first used in the mid-1990s that famously showed in several experiments that African American college freshmen and sophomores performed more poorly on standardized tests than Caucasian students when their race was emphasized. When race was not emphasized, however, African American students performed better and more equivalently with Caucasian students. The results showed that performance in academic contexts can be harmed by the awareness that one's behavior might be viewed through the lens of racial stereotypes.

The consequences of stereotype threat extend beyond underachievement on academic tasks. For example, it can lead to self-handicapping strategies such as reduced practice time for a task. In addition, consistent exposure to stereotype threat (e.g., faced by some ethnic minorities in academic environments, women in math, and dumb jocks who know everything about sports but care little about excelling in the classroom) can reduce the degree that individuals value the domain in question. In education, it can also lead students choosing not to pursue a particular major or course of study and consequently limit the range of professions that they can pursue. Therefore, the long-term effects of stereotype threat might contribute to educational and social inequality. Furthermore, stereotype threat has been shown to affect stereotyped individuals' performance in a number of areas beyond academics– including women in negotiation, homosexual men in providing childcare, and even Asians in driving situations.

> *Athletes, as individuals, are some of the most vulnerable to stereotype threat. The academic achievement gap between athletes and non-athletes at many high schools and colleges can be explained by athletes simply psyching themselves into below-average performance. Research has shown that stereotype threat can harm the academic performance of any individual for whom the situation invokes a stereotype-based expectation of poor performance.*

In addition, research also demonstrates that within a stereotyped group, some members may be more vulnerable to its negative consequences than others; factors such as the strength of one's group identification (like football or hockey vs. water polo and tennis) or position identification (like quarterback vs. defensive lineman) have been shown to be related to ones' subsequent vulnerability to stereotype threat. As a result, at some schools, while athletes in some sports consistently out-perform the general student body, athletes in other sports may suffer dearly because of a deeply-rooted legacy of under performance by its athletes.

Student-Athletes Face a Tough Task: 'Role Strain'

While most of what transpires in college athletics is positive, there is a growing sense among academic leaders, the news media, and the public that our society glorifies athletic accomplishment far more than academic achievement. The increasingly commercialized nature of major sports at the highest competitive levels, and a widening gulf between the athletic and academic cultures at some institutions, threaten to negatively affect the reputation and public standing of athletes as a whole. This is also creating 'role strain' for many athletes.

The athletic-academic relationship in the university setting has historically been problematic. This is the case because the assumption that sports are anti-intellectual pervades certain academic cultures. Because the dumb jock stereotype remains prevalent, student-athletes are often not seen as serious students. Consequently, some members of faculty may have lowered academic expectations of them. This stereotype, combined with the intrinsic and extrinsic gratification they receive for their athletic participation, makes it easier for many student-athletes to prioritize athletics above academics.

Over the course of their collegiate experience, many student-athletes tend to immerse themselves almost entirely in their athletic role (role engulfment) while simultaneously detaching themselves from their academic commitments (role abandonment).

> *When individuals are expected to fill multiple roles, they can experience role strain, in which commitment to one role detracts from the commitment to another. Student-athletes sometime experience role strain because of the competing time and energy demands of the athletic, social, and academic roles. But athletic, social, and academic roles need not be in conflict, as activities can be expanded or contracted depending upon the degree of commitment to a given role. Individuals can therefore make time and energy for multiple roles if they are committed to each of them.*

There are four ideal types of students based on the relative degree of commitment to each role:

1. The scholar-athlete,
2. The pure athlete,
3. The pure scholar, and
4. The non-scholar/non-athlete.

The athletic and academic roles of a student-athlete may be compatible, and in many cases they are, but it is important to know which type of academic and athletic role identities you possess.

The **scholar-athlete** demonstrates a high degree of commitment to both the athletic and academic role. In this case, the two domains are not in conflict. Rather than experiencing role strain, the scholar-athlete experiences an expansion of energy to meet the demands of both roles.

The **pure athlete** is almost wholly committed to the athletic role with almost no commitment to academics. Here, there may be role strain, where the commitment to athletics leaves little or no energy for academics. These pure athletes (often participants in the high-profile, revenue-producing sports) run the risk of failing academically or merely staying academically eligible to play their sport. Many of these student-athletes with a disproportionately high representation of minority and lower-income students produce annual revenues for their college teams well in excess of their athletic grant-in-aid. When these same student-athletes do not graduate, universities and their athletic departments are then accused of social and economic exploitation.

The **pure scholar** represents the converse of the pure athlete, where the commitment to the academic role leaves no time or energy for athletics.

Finally, the **non-scholar/non-athlete** is committed to neither role. This type of student may be committed to other extracurricular activities such as music, computers, etc.

Regardless of what type of student-traits you possess, student-athletes at most colleges and universities face a quantum leap in the athletic demands placed upon them. As a number of athletes have put it: "In high school, my sport was fun; now it's work." The academic expectations are likewise much more challenging, requiring a concerted effort just to maintain the minimum academic eligibility.

The time and energy obligations of college sports now require student-athletes to learn to manage their time more effectively and to study more efficiently. Thus, university student-athletes– even those with strong academic skills and a developed academic identity– must respond to these increased demands by making an even stronger commitment to academics and by expanding the time and mental energy devoted to academics.

> *The goal of most athletes will be to strike the proper balance between academic, social, and athletic demands that are often in conflict. Since most student-athletes come to the university with a strong athletic identity, the primary task facing most student-athletes is figuring out how best to develop or strengthen an academic identity while simultaneously maintaining a strong athletic commitment. This balancing act, which clearly requires conscious and persistent effort, is no easy trick.*

Balancing Academics vs. Athletics: Part 1

The academically successful student-athletes appear to be able to respond to the increased demands and transfer the qualities of hard work, discipline, and perseverance– all necessary traits for successful athletic performance and fulfilling academic lives. For these students, academics and athletics complement and reinforce one another.

In fact, some student-athletes actually do better academically when their sport is in season and report that the time and energy demands of athletics provide the necessary incentive to become more focused and efficient. As a result, a well-developed academic identity, which is reflected in strong academic self-worth, plays a critical role in academic success. A stable belief in the ability to compete academically at the university and a strong academic identity fuel the driving motivation needed to attain academic excellence. In these cases, as in real life, success breeds success, just as continuous failure breeds failure.

The academically marginal student-athletes respond less successfully to the increased demands of college. These student-athletes fail to make the connection between the behaviors necessary for athletic success and those necessary for academic success. They have weak academic identities and strong athletic identities due in part to a history of excessive emphasis on athletics at the expense of academic effort. This often results in poor academic preparation, less academic self-worth, and less academic motivation.

These student-athletes appear unwilling to make the necessary extra commitment to academics. Rather than working harder to meet increased demands and to compensate for their academic deficiencies, they respond to this role strain by passively allowing the athletic role to engulf them. This athletic engulfment reduces their motivation to achieve success within the academic sphere. The primary academic goal becomes merely staying eligible to compete athletically. Earning the minimum number of units and the requisite 2.0 grade point average becomes a short-term panacea for next season's competition.

When a combination of poor academic preparation and a greater commitment to athletics leads to poor academic performance, the student-athlete may then blame the mandated athletic demands for his or her poor performance rather than his or her own lack of academic effort. The lack of academic effort is disguised by adopting self-handicapping excuses for poor performance. This lack of commitment to academics eventually results in the student-athlete's failure to develop a strong academic identity and acquire the knowledge, skills, and intellectual interest to be anything more than a marginal student.

> *The prevalent belief among certain student-athletes that they are being exploited by the university for their athletic ability provides yet another rationalization for poor performance, particularly because there is some justification for these feelings of resentment. These feelings of resentment are particularly salient for revenue athletes who are often keenly aware of the potential income generated as a result of their athletic labor.*

As these intercollegiate athletes come to realize that their prospects of turning professional are slim, some student-athletes believe that the university is using their athletic ability without providing the support necessary for them to become successful students. Unfortunately, the realization that they must pursue a career other than professional sports often arrives too late for many of these individuals to refocus their energies. In response, many of these student-athletes expend the minimal effort academically, achieving only the bare minimum they need to remain athletically eligible. The subsequent lack of confidence in their ability to compete academically becomes a self-fulfilling prophecy and robs these individuals of an enriching college experience.

Balancing Academics vs. Athletics: Part 2

Student-athletes present an apparent motivational contradiction. They are highly motivated to succeed in the athletic domain, yet many seem to lack such motivation in the classroom. This apparent lack of academic motivation is reflected in a general misidentification with school and reduced academic performance.

In order to be a successful athlete, an individual must be willing to work hard, exhibit perseverance and determination, and remain focused. It would seem that these behaviors, if transferred to the academic domain, would ensure academic success. However, many student-athletes appear either unable or unwilling to make this transfer and are much less successful as students than as athletes. Differences in intrinsic motivation, external rewards, and social influences favoring athletics provide some of the explanation for this seeming paradox.

The self-worth theory of achievement motivation also provides a motivational explanation, which can contribute to our understanding of this discrepancy between academic and athletic motivation. The self-worth theory "assumes that the search for self-acceptance is the highest human priority, and self-acceptance comes to depend on one's ability to achieve competitively." Self-worth is therefore determined by an individual's own perception of their ability, as well as the perception of others– and these perceptions are mainly tied to successful achievement.

Success demonstrates competence or ability, thus enhancing self-worth. In competitive situations where success is limited to a select few individuals, the first priority for those who fear they may not be successful is the avoidance of failure and its implication that one lacks ability or competence. Trying hard and still failing leads to a questioning of one's ability, which, in turn, diminishes one's self-worth. On the other hand, failure following a lack of effort does not reflect negatively on one's ability and self-worth. This lack of effort leaves open the potential for future success and provides an excuse for failure that leaves the perception of ability and self-worth intact.

> *Have you ever heard your coach say something like, "You're not trying hard enough. What are you afraid of... failure?" A lack of effort can also be disguised and rationalized by self-handicapping excuses such as procrastination, test anxiety, and last-minute or inadequate study or preparation. In the classroom, heavily recruited and academically under-prepared student-athletes may be prone to reduce academic effort and employ these self-handicapping excuses while putting all of their effort into athletics where they know they can be personally successful, regardless of team performance, and enhance their own self-worth.*

🎾 The Choices You Make Stay With You a Lifetime

As we discussed earlier, highly competitive athletes may experience a series of emotional, physical, social, and mental changes during a transition to *CareerBall*... changes that will have different intensity and impact depending on the individual. Coping mechanisms may include denial, isolation, substance abuse, or other negative behaviors. Retirement from sports is not easy, even if the athlete is ready. But a transition that is prepared for and welcomed, however, will usually generate less stress than one that is viewed negatively or approached poorly.

Career development is such an important aspect of life. Over the years, a ton of research has been conducted to explain the significance of career development. From the time we enter this world until the day we die, we will experience changes. Circumstances and unplanned events will force us to make informed (and some crazy) decisions about our career choices.

As you age, and at different stages throughout your life, there will be many factors that may contribute to and impact your career choices. These factors can fall into several categories including environmental, personal, family, financial, and health-related issues. Where you live, where you grew up, what your parents did for a living, who has influenced you, your money motivations, and physical capabilities are all in play when you make career choices.

Career development also involves being acutely aware of one's personal goals, values, and work goals. It involves continuously learning and applying new knowledge, taking advantage of opportunities, and taking risks in order to increase effectiveness and productivity on a personal level and for your organization.

> *Athletes are somewhat at a disadvantage to the non-athlete at the critical time of identifying the initial career signals. Why? Countless college athletes have asked me, "Who has the time to worry about tomorrow when I'm head-down working out and competing and being the best I can be today!" I'll try to be nice here, but this viewpoint isn't just being clueless... it's pathologically dumb.*

Are You a "Tunnel Vision" Athlete?

If you are presently going through your high school or college life or squeaking by in the pros somewhere and you see sports as 100% of your self-image, there is a little thing called tunnel vision that you need to learn about. In medical terms, tunnel vision is "the loss of peripheral vision with the retention of central vision, resulting in a constricted circular tunnel-like field of vision." Focus on something long enough, and after a while, that's all you see.

Medically, tunnel vision can be caused by the following things, among others:

- ✓ Blood Loss or alcohol consumption
- ✓ Hallucinogenic drugs or glaucoma
- ✓ An intense physical fight, intense anger, or extreme fear or distress
- ✓ The ever-so-common bite from a Black Mamba

In highly competitive athletes, tunnel vision can be caused also by:

- ✓ Constantly being told by friends, family, coaches, and yourself what a great athlete you are
- ✓ Becoming addicted to popularity or getting your name on SportsCenter,
- ✓ Being CLUELESS that there is more to life than just being a terrific athlete

The consequences of tunnel vision can be fatal. Don't believe me? Think about it in cases of piloting an aircraft, driving, or operating heavy machinery... or spending a lifetime perfecting your athletic skills to the exclusion of most everything else. This sort of limitation can kill off your chances for a rewarding career.

If you have tunnel vision, it may be hereditary. Perhaps it began early in your sports participation, where the intensity level reached a certain point and your parents moved into tunnel vision, literally losing sight of what is important in youth sports and focusing narrowly on you and how you handle that ball, to the exclusion of everything else.

Bottom line is, nothing good comes from tunnel vision. If you suspect you might have it, the time to own up and deal with this reality is NOW… starting today!

Dumb Jock or Scholar-Athlete?... Your Choice

When most people talk about the social groups in their school, they matter-of-factly categorize almost every fellow student into stereotyped pigeonholes. There are the nerds, the Greeks, the rockers, the preppies, the Goths– and of course, the jocks.

> *Everyone knows the term jock is derived from the word jockstrap, which hardly anybody still wears, but the term has stuck. The term jock is a classic North American stereotype of a male athlete, but with the recent rise in women sports, women have felt the sting of this ugly stereotype as well. Odd, since women don't even use jockstraps!*

The jock stereotype is attributed mostly to high school and college athletes who form a significant youth subculture.

As a blanket term, "the jock" is considered synonymous with an athlete, and the jock stereotype is used often in the mass media to portray a relatively unintelligent and unenlightened, but nonetheless physically and socially well-endowed character.

The list of negative stereotypical characteristics of a jock includes:

- ✓ Muscular/athletic, but conversely not considered intelligent
- ✓ Popular among classmates or students similar to his own clique
- ✓ Generally homophobic
- ✓ Generally popular with the girls, but is often despised by non-jock boys
- ✓ Competitive
- ✓ Prone to being cruel, mean, and bullying.
- ✓ Usually a very attractive girlfriend (typically a cheerleader) but shows signs of disrespect toward women (abuse, crude sexual jokes, etc.)

And here's the one that I despise the most:

- ✓ Often perceived as getting preferential treatment solely due to athletic ability (e.g., passing grades undeserved, bad conduct overlooked)

One Bad Apple Spoils the Whole Bunch

In our society, there is a very real distinction between the label "athlete" and "jock." When most people hear the term "jock," they think of an athlete who is dumb. When they hear "athlete," they typically make no intelligence assumption at all; or perhaps out of a vague sense of respect, they may be inclined to assume high intelligence. This is one of the reasons athletes in college are referred to as student-athletes and why you should always refer to yourself as an athlete, not a jock, when talking about your experience and skills with potential employers.

To be fair, there are dumb jocks out there just as there are scholar-athletes, pure-athletes, or student-athletes. The fact of the matter is that not all athletes are necessarily dumb– though some of the dumb people happen to be athletes. They might have even been a minority of the athlete population, but they stood out for their stellar stupidity.

A lot of athletes (particularly at the high-school level) also treat other members of the student body very badly. As a coping mechanism, many non-athletes assume that all athletes must be jocks and that all jocks must be must be stupid and will end up digging ditches or pumping gas for a living down the road– not that there is anything wrong with ditch-digging or gas-pumping if that is the career choice you want to take.

> *The good news is that times have changed for many athletes, and the term "dumb jock" now says more about the last century than this century. As the competition increases for admission to major universities, eligibility requirements for athletes to participate continues to rise, and with more and more studies demonstrating that athletic participation is associated with higher academic performance, why does the dumb jock stereotype persist? It really isn't much different than the stereotype that all blonds are dumb. Where did that come from and why does it persist?*

I believe these stereotypes have persisted for many reasons and are tough to break or change public opinion. For one, media doesn't help. The dumb jock is still being written into movies, television shows, and cartoons, and even in an intelligent society such as ours, people have a tendency to think that what happens on a sitcom is a depiction of real life. Another reason could possibly be jealousy. Some people just don't or won't believe that a person could have it all– brains, beauty, and athletic ability.

I think the dumb jock stereotype may also be a reaction against the fact that athletes may be (or may appear to be) more cliquish than other stereotypes, not to mention the fact that sports figures are held in such high esteem– even by adults. Athletes may feel privileged and entitled in a way that is disproportionate to their talents, especially academically. Also, because sports teams comprise such a big part of a school's self-esteem, some athletes have felt they can get away with anything and not suffer consequences just because they are "stars"– and sadly, this is often the case.

It is also important to look at professional sports if we're talking about a sports stereotype. Since they draw the most public attention, they set the precedent. The thing is, more and more pro athletes don't graduate from college. They either skip school entirely, or they enter the draft before their senior year. Are they gainfully employed? Yes. Does that make them smart? No. And sadly, there are still plenty of dumb jocks in professional sports. Seemingly every other week, some professional athlete is busted carrying a loaded gun into a nightclub, driving their sports car at 150 MPH, or lying to Congress about their appetite for performance-enhancing drugs. Irresponsible off-field behavior is always made an example of these days, and as long as athletes are human, there will always be examples of dumb jocks.

Whatever the reason people feel compelled to stereotype athletes as jocks, all athletes share in the responsibility to break the public perception of the dumb jock. If you think you fit the general description of a dumb jock, it's time to begin the process to change your behavior and come kicking and screaming into the twenty-first century.

However, at the end of the day, the typical athlete isn't the proverbial dumb football player who majors in stained glass. Typically, student-athletes as a whole out-perform their non-athlete peers in college; they earn better grades and enjoy a higher graduation rate. As a result, the term "scholar-athlete" is gaining in popularity, both as a stereotype and as a calling– a status that is viewed as desirable to athletes themselves, their parents and, best of all, employers.

The Trend is Improving

In Division I sports at NCAA schools, student-athletes are graduating at the highest rates ever, according to the latest NCAA Graduation Success Rates (GSR). The most recent GSR data show that 79% of freshmen student-athletes who entered college earned their four-year degrees. The average Graduation Success Rate for the last four graduating classes is 79%. Using the federal government's methodology for calculating graduation rates, which does not count transfer students and is less accurate than the GSR, Division I student-athletes who entered college graduated at 64%, still the highest federal rate ever and one point higher than the general student body.

The NCAA leadership has praised the latest GSR figures, citing increased initial-eligibility standards and an overall emphasis on academics, including the development of the Academic Progress Rate (APR) for each Division I sports team as key factors contributing to student-athlete success. The APR tracks academic progress of its athletes on each NCAA team.

The net result is that nearly eight out of ten Division I student-athletes are finishing college and earning their degrees. Academically speaking, the so called "dumb jock" myth is becoming just that– a myth.

🎾 The 'Dark Side' of Highly Competitive Athletes

While there are many positive qualities that shape the athlete DNA, beware of the agro-athlete who lives in the world of hyper-competitiveness. One of the principle characteristics of a competitive athlete (and one of the most confusing) is aggressive behavior.

While you might have been rewarded and encouraged for aggressive behavior in practices and games, remember that the work environment (especially in interviews) is not the best place to go agro. Aggressive people tend to be offensive to bosses and threatening to individuals that do not possess or understand the competitive athlete DNA. Over-amped individuals also make pests of themselves.

It will be important to remember that you are being asked to tone-down perhaps fifteen to twenty years of competitive conditioning. In some cases, you will need to function as if the polar opposite of what you have been taught is true– in job search activities and jobs themselves, being purposeful, persistent, and pleasant is the rewarded behavior.

🎾 Are You an "Alpha Personality?"

Athletes can best be described as bold, self-confident, and demanding of themselves and their teammates. Athletes tend to get things done, but the DNA traits that make them so productive can also drive others crazy.

Athletes that are highly intelligent, confident, and successful are oftentimes described as Alpha males or Alpha females. As the label implies, they're the people who aren't happy unless they are the top dogs– the ones clearly calling the shots.

> *Alphas reach the top ranks in large organizations because they are natural leaders. They will be comfortable with responsibility in a way non-Alphas can never be. Most people feel stress when they have to make important decisions: Alphas get stressed when tough decisions don't rest in their capable hands. For them, being in charge delivers such a thrill that they willingly take on levels of responsibility most rational people would find overwhelming. In fact, it's hard to imagine a successful sports team or the modern corporation without Alpha leaders in place.*

Most Alphas assess information and situations very quickly, and this rapid processing can prevent them from listening to others– especially to those who don't communicate in "Alpha-speak." Their impatience can thus cause them to miss subtle but important details. Alphas, moreover, have opinions about everything, and they rarely admit that those opinions might be wrong or incomplete. Early in life, Alphas realize that they are smarter than most people– perhaps even smarter than their parents and teachers; as adults, they believe that their insights are unique and therefore put complete faith in their instincts and expect others to do the same.

Because their intuitions are so often proven right, Alphas feel justified in focusing on the flaws in other people's ideas or arguments. As a result, co-workers and teammates get intimidated, which makes learning from Alphas difficult. The more pressure an Alpha feels to perform, the more he or she tends to shift their leadership style from constructive and challenging to intimidating or even abusive. At its worst, organizations become dysfunctional when people avoid dealing with a difficult Alpha and instead work around him or her or simply pay them lip service.

Alphas:

- ✓ Tend to be emotional and analytical in their cognitive style, and as a result, they are eager to learn about business, technology, and "things" but have little or no natural curiosity about people or feelings.

- ✓ Tend to rely on exhaustive data to reach business conclusions and then often make snap judgments about people, their skills and value, and then hold on tenaciously with their opinions.

- ✓ Tend to believe that paying attention to feelings, even their own, detracts from getting the job done, and as a result, they're surprisingly oblivious to the effects they have on others.

- ✓ Tend to judge teammates or colleagues who cannot control their emotions, yet often fail to notice how they project their own anger and frustration. Or they dismiss their own outbursts, arguing that the same rules should not apply to top dog.

- ✓ Tend to find it difficult to ask for help or even to acknowledge that they need it, and as a result, they typically are stubborn and resistant to feedback. After all, they haven't gotten where they are by being self reflective.

- ✓ Tend to be generally clueless when it comes to the effects of their personality. As much as they love talking about accountability, they often fail to see that their own communication style, rather than someone else's shortcomings, is what creates the roadblocks on the team or in the office. As a result, they're uncomfortable showing vulnerability or taking a break from constant action.

What About Alpha Females?

Although there are plenty of successful female leaders with equally strong personalities, top women rarely (if ever) match the complete Alpha profile of the male athlete.

Ask people to identify Alpha males, and they'll readily produce a list. But ask them if they work with or know any Alpha females, and they'll look confused. "Are those the really smart women– the ones who are best at getting things done– or are they the bossy ones?" they might ask you. It's easy to identify successful female leaders but often harder to categorize them. In my work with athletes, I've encountered many women who possess some of the traits of the Alpha male, but none who possess all of them.

> *Women can be just as data-driven and opinionated as Alpha males and can cope with stress equally well, but the vast majority of women place more value on interpersonal relationships and pay closer attention to people's feelings. Women at the top are generally comfortable with control and being in charge, but they don't seek to dominate people and situations as Alpha males do. Although equally talented, ambitious, and hardheaded, they often rise to positions of authority by excelling at collaboration, and they are less inclined to resort to intimidation to get what they want. Female leaders are more likely to use a "velvet hammer," tending to express orders as polite suggestions.*

Like Alpha males, some Alpha female leaders do have problems with anger and bullying, and they can be defensive and resistant to criticism. However, the work environment (and society as a whole) is much less tolerant of these negative characteristics in women than in men. As a result, far fewer women with these tendencies ever reach executive positions.

Because women more readily understand the importance of positive motivation and the limitations of fear-driven cultures, they are less likely to avoid interpersonal issues. They may not enjoy delving into the touchy-feely zones anymore than Alpha males do, but they are more willing to so because they understand that inspiring and motivating people are just as important as pursuing the right ideas.

Female leaders are less comfortable with conflict, while Alpha males thrive on it. When the Alpha male doesn't like something, he states it loudly and clearly. A female leader can be less willing to force an issue publicly if she doesn't anticipate quick assent. Being more interested in collaborating and finding win-win solutions, she'll happily debate an idea until someone's emotions are triggered, at which point she'll typically back down rather than press toward resolution. This indirect style of communication is often misinterpreted by male peers; in fact, some female leaders have been accused by peers of being political and having hidden agendas. Strong women leaders should be aware that their indirect style can engender distrust among certain kinds of men. If you are a female, remember that what you call "diplomacy," your male counterpart may call "politics."

If You Think You Might Be an Alpha Athlete...

Here's Five Steps Toward Alpha Growth

If you have concluded you might be an Alpha leader, here is some food for thought on what it will take to fit more comfortably in the workplace after your playing days are over.

> *To change, the Alpha athletes (who become Alpha leaders) must become more aware of their own motivations, more open to their peers' contrary opinions, and more comfortable with public challenge. Scary thought, but you must also learn to deliver feedback that is useful rather than traumatic. If you see yourself as an Alpha, focus on these five goals that will help you become a motivational leader rather than a cage fighter:*

1. Admit vulnerability.

When Alphas admit they are afraid or ask for help, the impact on their team is profoundly positive. Disclosing your imperfections will be an uncomfortable stretch, but that action will humanize you in the eyes of the team and make you more inspirational to the rest of the organization. When you disclose the traits you are working to improve, it helps convince your team that you are serious about changing.

2. Accept accountability.

Alphas tend to feel very accountable for their own performance, but they have difficulty accepting responsibility for their impact on other people's performance. Until you accept ownership for your share of a problem, problems will not get corrected. Paradoxically, when you admit you're wrong and need to change, you will come across as more confident and courageous than when you insisted you were always right.

3. Connect with underlying emotions.

The Alpha doesn't like emotions because they cannot be controlled, and they believe emotions impede logic and impair decision-making. If this is your attitude, you have a lot of work to do. You probably are somewhat out of touch with your feelings so much so that when you're not in control, anger is the likely emotion to pop out. And beneath that anger often lurks other emotions such as fear and disappointment. It is important for you to learn to recognize your underlying emotions while you are still at the gut level, long before the big eruption occurs.

4. Balance positive with critical feedback.

Alphas feel uncomfortable both giving and receiving praise, and they are adamant about not appearing soft. A strong manager, they say, is comfortable "telling it like it is." As a result, about 80% of the conversations with an Alpha leader will contain critical comments. Underlying the Alpha's reluctance to express appreciation is a self-perception that they do not require (or respond to) positive feedback. People reflexively react to criticism with defensiveness and resistance, whereas a balance of positive and negative feedback is more likely to motivate people to change. You must be careful to express your positive feelings towards teammates and coworkers, restating your appreciation several times with different wordings so that people really get it. Anything short of this strategy will be viewed as disingenuous or even patronizing– both of which are not very flattering to you.

5. Become aware of patterns.

People tend to slip into a whole set of dramatic, predictable roles that spring from the family, sports, and school dynamics in which they grew up. Many interpersonal problems in the workplace stem from the past, and they create the behind-the-scenes lobbying, venting, and complaining that characterizes so many organizations. It is well-known that most everyone sees themselves through the personality roles they take on or possess– and how others see them as well. Here are a few typical personas that you might know:

➢ The **Athlete** persona, who typically views others as either winners or losers.

➢ The **Rebel** persona, who typically sees the world as full of people to be acted against.

➢ The **Boss** persona, who typically thinks the world needs supervision and discipline.

➢ The **Bulldozer** persona, who typically plows through people if they think that's what's needed to get the right thing done.

➢ The **Complaining Victim** persona, who typically withholds good ideas and hard work because they don't want to get run over by the Bulldozer.

To get around this problem, Alphas need to recognize that any extreme behavior or reoccurring pattern signifies that they have fallen into one of their personas, and they need to become more conscious of their behavior and its effect on others.

Do You Need Help?

Smart athletes and smart non-athletes know when to take the time and pay close attention to their academic, athletic, and personal well being. It is far too important to jeopardize by not getting help when it is needed to keep yourself in balance. Role strain, social stigmas, and competitive pressure to perform in the classroom and on the field, are but a few of the many negative forces that affect highly competitive athletes, and it is very important to seek help for problems and situations that you cannot figure out yourself.

But being an athlete sometimes also creates an internal block to seeking out the very help that is necessary and healthy for a balanced life. Some of the reasons why athletes might not seek help, include:

✓ Many athletes are high visibility students and often stand out on-campus. This may make it difficult for them to blend in and receive services just like any other student.

✓ Because student-athlete schedules are filled with academic and athletic responsibilities, they often have little free time in their schedules to use services that are generally only open during traditional office hours.

✓ Many student-athletes are led to believe, sometimes correctly, but often not, that the athletic department will meet all their needs. Student-athletes who believe this may see the general student services as irrelevant or simply as duplications of what they can get in the athletic department

- ✓ Various personal characteristics, that have likely helped you succeed in your sport, such as being highly self-reliant, may stop you from seeking help from others. In addition, some student-athletes believe that a good athletic performance can solve all their problems, avoiding more direct and effective solutions that might be available to them.

- ✓ Many student-athletes share the stereotype that anyone who sees a counselor or asks someone else for help is either crazy or weak. Perhaps because of this widespread stereotype, many student-athletes are reluctant to seek counseling because they are afraid of being put down by others.

In any event, it's the smart individual who understands the types of strains that come with being a competitive athlete and also seeks out professional assistance when they are faced with problems and situations they cannot figure out themselves. Are you a "smart athlete" or a "dumb jock"?

Chapter 3

Why Athletes Make Great Employees!

Interpreting and Leveraging Your Athlete "Soft Skills"

In my opinion, athletics is one of the few remaining bastions in our society which can help mold such badly needed personal characteristics of self-discipline, rugged determination, self-control in times of stress, unselfishness, good sportsmanship, and fair play.

Whether they realize it or not, highly competitive athletes have acquired the abilities and discipline that allow them to focus on whatever is in front of them, to complete whatever task is at hand, whether it is taking a pitch to the opposite field or writing a computer program. This may have come as a result of running in endless baseball fungo drills, basketball layup lines, or stroke timing sessions on a crew boat. When companies hire, they always look for those that offer physical stamina, mental toughness, and razor-sharp concentration. Companies look for that passion, that concentration, that inner tension in men and women who know what it's like to fail and get up and try again.

The fundamental truth of athletics in our society is the belief that trained athletes, as a group, have achieved exposure to high-level success, and, as a result, will tend to exceed the general population in a variety of important social and performance disciplines. Experience and training in teamwork, goal setting, time management, punctuality, discipline, initiative, drive, and loyalty are some of the many skills attributed to athletes in high levels of competition. This experience is an attractive common denominator in top job performance across all industry segments.

> *In sports and in organizations, pressure, deadlines and competition are commonplace. Sports give players the experience of dealing with these realities and learning to enjoy and conquer their challenges. When there are only two seconds left on the clock, your team is one point down, and you go up for the jump shot, you learn what pressure, deadlines, and competition are all about and how that can be perceived as exhilarating and fun rather than scary and distasteful. The bottom line is that most organizations want to hire people who enjoy and excel in competitive environments.*

The workforce in the United States has oftentimes sought a particular athletic or extracurricular background of job candidates as one of the few common identifying attributes of previously successful employees. It is no secret that success breeds success in the workplace, and athletes who have withstood and met the rigorous standards of maintaining eligibility are considered to be successful individuals, regardless of specific athletic accomplishments. It is also a fact that many hiring managers, department leaders, senior managers, and industry leaders enjoy rigorous and successful athletic experiences at the collegiate level prior to entering the workforce. This "takes one to know one" experience is not only a great common denominator in the interview process, but these individuals really understand what special skills athletes bring to their jobs.

There is also a positive correlation between an individual's level of income and collegiate athletic participation. It has been verified that athletic participation produces personal traits or behavior patterns that enhance labor market productivity or that athletes acquire a work ethic that increases employer demand for their services off the playing field. This is a fancy way to say that athletes oftentimes earn more money than non-athletes in the workplace.

Ultimately, participation in sports teaches athletes all about the foundation of a strong work ethic: that hard work, repetition, and constant practice, are the keys to successful performance. Athletes know that no matter how tired they are, they can tap into a reservoir of stamina, strength, and clear thinking– even under the most difficult of circumstances– and continue to compete successfully and produce results.

What Can Athlete DNA Do in the Workforce?

I believe (as most organizations do) that motivated, directed, self aware athletes can achieve quality-driven results when measured against clearly established goals– and much more so than non-athletes. I call this the "Won-Loss Effect."

Athletes who have competed at the college level or beyond possess a vast knowledge and experience and what it takes to compete and to win or lose. In athletics, there are rarely any ties; always a winner and loser, and by the time a college athlete completes their eligibility, they have amassed hundreds of win-lose situations where something was learned as a result of the outcome.

> *Highly competitive athletes are rarely satisfied with being mediocre and are always looking to better themselves. Once collegiate athletes hang up their cleats, they shift their attention to the workforce using the same principles that made them successful as a student-athlete. Athletes seldom lose the passion of always trying to improve themselves to get to the next level. Most people want to get to the next level but do nothing to get there; that is what makes athletes truly elite, because they know what it takes to get to the top.*

Athletes have a basis of many years of training to achieve the best personal and/or team performance they can throughout their career. Their tenacity and determination complement their will to succeed by performing the absolute best on an everyday basis. This noteworthy training and performance provide the athlete with an opportunity to identify areas for improvement and learn new skills.

Athletes that have competed at the college level understand firsthand that teamwork, development, and hands-on practice serve as a terrific supplement to the academic aptitude they earn in the classroom. Utilizing a strong work ethic and mental toughness, focused student-athletes develop well polished traits that are desired by organizations nationwide. Student-athletes have an ultimate desire for success in the work force because it fulfils the need to challenge, compete, and win!

Having worked with thousands of athletes that have made the successful transition to a career, I have observed a number of recurring facts that prove to me the belief that successful, highly competitive athletes are an asset to any workforce or career:

- ✓ First and foremost among these attributes is an individual's motivation level. If you were a motivated athlete, chances are you will carry that important skill into your career.

- ✓ Being a part of a team and competing competitively is one of the most important keys to success in the workplace. If you were on a team and enjoyed the experience, you will excel nicely in a career setting.

- ✓ Sports not only brings you into a teamwork atmosphere, but it also drives your work ethic at an early age. On a baseball diamond, for instance, you can quickly tell who has been working hard and who has been lazy. Sports brings out your leadership qualities, which, in turn, creates a sense of confidence for a person in the business world. Not all athletes are just "dumb jocks," and they deserve respect in the business world; because many of them maintained a very high GPA in school while practicing some type of sport at least thirty hours a week– no easy feat.

- ✓ One of the greatest perspectives you have probably gained as a competitive athlete is the understanding very early in life of what hard work, dedication, and believing in your dream actually means, as well as how your participation can benefit the larger group.

- ✓ Sports may build character, but I suggest that people bring the character that is already formed within them to their sports activity, rather than the other way around. If you were a successful athlete, it's because you already had character in the first place. In my experience, however, team sports in many ways do help shape your character.

- ✓ In sports, winning is everything, and this competitive spirit may inevitably devolve into abusive behavior and a "win at any cost" mentality. You may not agree with that, but in the absence of any definitive studies on the subject, I believe that winning does not always equate to the better person or better group of individuals. Winning, after all, is a surrogate for survival. The best survivor wins. So, business success derived from sports participation means we've bred a better predator. Sports can be viewed as socially acceptable predatory behavior.

- ✓ In my experience, leadership and the concept of teamwork aren't bestowed solely upon the most talented athletes. In fact, the greatest captains/leaders

I've worked with were not their team's most gifted or outstanding players. It was always apparent to me who were the difference-makers in the locker room, on the bench, and on the field of competition.

- ✓ Interestingly, it's often hard to qualify what "success" is as athletes move forward into their working lives. I'd suggest that many of the athletes I've worked with have become enormously successful within their chosen field without necessarily becoming CEOs, renowned innovators, or independently wealthy. It is readily apparent that these athletes have learned valuable lessons from their participation in sports.

- ✓ When contacted by a potential employer about one of my athletes, I always comment that while I can't determine what that individual's aptitude is for the job in question, I can clearly and confidently comment about their core values, dedication, ability to handle adversity, honesty, integrity, loyalty, etc. Most often, the person on the other end of the phone is speechless. In a fifteen-minute phone conversation, they've learned more about that individual than a dozen interviews would have revealed.

- ✓ The sports environment is clearly a place where one develops rapport, and it's also a proving ground for the kinds of skills a leader needs.

- ✓ Athletes have become conditioned to a fast-paced, varied environment. Job burnout is a real risk for athletes, so selecting the "right" career and job interest is paramount to longevity and job satisfaction.

- ✓ I think there's a lot to be said for individuals who managed participating in sports with academics, with part-time jobs and/or family commitments. There are time-management skills involved, and certainly social development skills, not to mention confidence, self-esteem, and the ability to deal with difficult situations.

Common Traits Within the Athlete DNA

Abilities and motivations are the qualifications employers expect for particular jobs. Your motivated abilities and skills are generally a combination of your own particular DNA and the transferable skills you acquired during your years of sports participation. Since you are an unknown and risky quantity for a prospective employer, you must communicate evidence of these abilities and skills so they can better predict your future performance.

This is a "Which came first, the chicken or the egg?" kind of argument, for it is debatable whether it is athletic participation that allows athletes to develop the traits and skills that make them successful or if it is simply that people who participate in athletics inherently possess these traits. Regardless of the outcome of that debate, at the end of the day, athletes know how to win!

> *Employers look for signs of a future productivity when they look to hire someone. Typically, every great athlete possesses a few innate traits common to an athlete DNA that are known elements of a productive team environment and a high-level athletic environment. Here are eight DNA qualities your athletic experience has directly or indirectly taught you that will be very beneficial and transferable to the working world. Make certain all your future employers know you possess these qualities, and be prepared to cite personal examples where each quality was learned.*

1. Being Passionate and Positive

As an athlete, you have firsthand experience in finding your passion and working with the best and most positive people you can find. You have learned that focusing on the things you can control and not worrying about the things you cannot control is paramount to success. You have also learned the valuable experience of creating and being part of a team and being a part of a group of individuals who care as much about the people around them as they do about themselves– people who will work synergistically toward a common goal.

2. Motivation

As an athlete, you know about waking up nervous the day of a big event or practice and realizing that motivation to excel– to harness the excitement and energy for the day– is a fundamental key to success. You know that the drive to succeed often comes from inside yourself and not from any external influence. Fear is something that great athletes also face, but they overcome their fears and go out and compete anyway. Being motivated is about seeing the light, keeping your eyes on the prize and knowing why you want to make things happen. And when you reach success, you know it is not the time to rest on your laurels. You know the temptation to slack off starts when you're feeling good about who you are and what you've achieved… and you know that it takes significant motivation to not fall victim to this temptation.

3. Going Above and Beyond

Great athletes who people admire and respect are the ones who will go the extra mile. The same is true in order to be successful in business and to lead an enriching and satisfying life. As an athlete, it is not enough to do just the bare minimum to get by. You know that each day there is only one person who truly knows what level of effort you have put forth to be successful… you. And when you have stayed after practice to work on a particular skill, or left the party early so you can catch up on important sleep, or put away the X-Box in order to go to the gym, you have demonstrated and experienced the difficult quality of learning to go above and beyond what is required. This is an enormously important skill to possess.

4. Purpose

As an athlete, you possess a fundamental purpose underlying your success– a sense of purpose in what you have accomplished. And fundamental to this purpose is caring about other people, about being aware of what the people around you need. You have learned about helping teammates play better and compete intelligently. Maybe you came from an athletic program in which you didn't talk exclusively about winning, but also about life's great lessons. Maybe your athletic history has helped you see the constant quest to be the best you can be. For you, sports was more than just a game– it also provided you with a sense of purpose.

5. *Being Optimistic*

> *One of the favorite phrases in sports is "You never know." This is about being optimistic and trusting your instincts and never lying down until the last ounce of opportunity has been exhausted. As an athlete, you have learned that sometimes you have to go with a hunch, confidently knowing that your own optimism might be the only reason to take on a difficult challenge. It is also about treating everyone you meet and compete with, including referees and umpires, with the optimistic opinion that they are good, honest people. As an athlete, you learn to treat every situation as an opportunity.*

6. *Focus and Practice*

Great athletes become great by mastering the quality of remaining focused in their tasks, actions, and challenges. As an athlete, you know the value of being prepared and that without the discipline of practice, you run the risk of never achieving greater success or improving your individual skills. You know how to practice. Being focused and prepared includes knowing all you can about your sport… and ultimately, your profession. The more you know, the more you can do. The best athletes are always looking for ways to improve themselves.

7. *Opportunity in Adversity*

As an athlete, you have learned on a number of occasions that on the road to success, you're going to meet adversity and failure a few times. Great athletes overcome the naysayers and the odds. They adapt their goals to reality, and they never stop trying. Adversity is part of the road, and you have learned to accept it and keep going and to see the opportunity in the adversity.

You know that success is not a one-time incident. Success should be seen as a habit, and inside you can relate to the "champion mentality." To become a great athlete, you have experienced more success than you have failure in your life. In a way, you have become addicted to success. After you've reached a goal, you typically find a new challenge. Through sports, you have learned to pursue success in all aspects of your life.

8. *Good Enough is Not Enough*

As an athlete, you never become quite satisfied with the status quo. Inside your head, you know that nothing changes and nobody gets better if people accept that "good enough" is enough. You know how to stay out of the routine because routines don't help you grow. You have learned how to make little changes in how you improve yourself and your game, one at a time, and plan the next few as you go. As an athlete, you have experienced what it takes to make incremental and long-lasting changes so that you never feel comfortable with "good enough."

Valuable Currency that Counts

> We live in a skill-based society where individuals market their skills to employers in exchange for money, position, and power. As an athlete, you have acquired many skills through athletic competition that are transferable to the workplace and your career. Unfortunately, few athletes can identify and talk about their skills, even though they possess many different types of skills. This becomes a real problem when they must write a resume or present a good job interview. Since employers want to know about your specific abilities and skills, you must be able to both identify and communicate your skills. You should be able to explain what it is you do well and provide relevant examples directed at employers' needs.

Most people possess two distinct types of skills that define their competency strengths as well as enable them to enter and advance within the job market:

1. *Work content skills*
2. *Functional skills*

These skills become the key language for communicating your qualifications to employers in your resumes and letters as well as in interviews.

Work content skills are mainly acquired through experience rather than formal training and can be communicated through general vocabulary. Sometimes the title of your job is enough communicate work content skills, but generally, these skills involve doing things: repairing air-conditioners, building a house, developing a website, staffing a retail store, or cooking fast food. .

Functional transferable skills are less easy to recognize and are linked to a certain personal characteristics (energetic, intelligent, likeable) and the ability to deal with processes (communicating, problem-solving, or motivating). Many athletes may lack work content skills, but they possess numerous functional transferable skills. In contrast to work content skills, these functional skills can be transferred from one job to the next, one career to the next, and are very valuable to prospective employers.

A major objective of any good career development plan or successful job search is developing awareness of your functional skills so you can relate them to the job market.

10 Primary Traits Why Athletes Are Successful in the Workplace

There are many traits that are common within highly competitive athletes. In fact, there are over twenty-five of them. But there are ten principle characteristics that define the athlete skill set and are components of excellent team players. These are also the ten primary characteristics that companies look for in making their hiring decisions.

These ten traits are largely acquired through a combination of personal life experiences including academic, athletic, social, and whatever previous community, volunteer, or work experiences you possess. When you have exhibited many of these important characteristics and can effectively communicate examples, you not only show great life balance to prospective employers, but you can also leverage your life experiences and your strengths and demonstrate exactly why you are destined for future success– and why you should be the one they hire.

> *Take a close look at these principle traits listed below. How many of these characteristics do you possess? Check (9) the box beside each characteristic that is strongly descriptive of you.* **Then circle the TOP THREE characteristics that are your real strengths:**

☐ **Ability to organize time well.**

As a well-rounded student, you participated in extracurricular activities like athletics, Greek, or other student organizations, social functions, and a full academic load. The commitment to athletics (which oftentimes includes year-round participation, travel to other schools for games and other team activities) requires a refined development of time management skills… to remain eligible, to compete effectively, to graduate and, most importantly, so you don't get in trouble with the coach.

☐ **Ability to work well with others**.

As a student, your "teaming" experiences within group projects goes a long way. Through athletic team membership, most student-athletes become very familiar with the experience of working toward group goals. Teaming experiences teach that sometimes it is necessary to submerge one's ego and personal goals into the goals of the organization, and that leadership is the ability to get people to work as a team.

☐ **Goal directedness.**

As a student, one must maintain focus despite distractions to succeed academically. Student-athletes develop the ability to concentrate their energies and attention over an extended period of time to block out distractions while they proceed toward their goals. Whether it is staying on an academic graduation track, managing a four-month competition season, or increasing your individual skills, the ability of staying on-goal is very valuable to employers.

☐ *Competitiveness.*

Competitive spirit is the lifeblood of the collegiate athletics experience. Student-athletes gain experience in the rigors of winning and losing, and they look forward to the opportunity to fight more battles, test their abilities, and risk their self-esteem against tough opposition. This is a strong asset in most jobs.

☐ *Confidence.*

The candidate with the athlete skill set has continually been in situations where they must pump up and believe in their own power to produce effectively under pressure. The ability to approach tough performance situations with the belief that you'll do well is crucial. Practice in maintaining self-confidence (especially under tense circumstances) can carry over to on-the-job challenges.

☐ *Persistence and endurance.*

These characteristics are often characterized by long and hard work toward distant rewards and the ability to wring a maximum effort from yourself whenever necessary. As a student, this may mean overcoming a difficult personal experience. As an athlete, it may include playing while in pain or performing under other adverse circumstances. The candidate with the athlete skill set believes intensity of effort and sufficient preparation and determination will eventually pay off.

☐ *Loyalty.*

Loyalty emerges from the bond that an individual builds with an organization, a team, or to another individual and is expressed in the willingness to support team efforts under any circumstances. Loyalty contributes to the morale of a team or work group because it enables each team member to trust that others will work toward the same ends. Since you come from the world of athletics, which is an organizational culture that values loyalty and teamwork, you are more likely to fit in a multitude of organizational cultures in the work world.

☐ *Discipline.*

Organizing one's time, adhering to guidelines, giving maximum effort on a regular basis, concentrating one's energies, and screening out competing priorities are all necessary in being a successful student or successful athlete. The systematic application of one's energies toward a desired goal is highly valued in any work setting.

☐ *Ability to take criticism.*

Because their performance on the field is watched closely, student-athletes are accustomed to taking criticism. Good coaches recommend changes and develop in their athletes the ability to cope with the feeling that they could have done better. Athletes typically develop into good listeners when constructive criticism is offered because they recognize its value in helping them advance toward overall goals.

☐ *Resilience.*

Certain life experiences, as well as college sports, can offer continued opportunities to test yourself and then come back for more, whether you succeed or fail. No one who competes in a sport can avoid the experience of failure. Student-athletes learn to face failure and bury any negative feelings because tomorrow's contest demands their full attention. Among the most valuable lessons of collegiate athletics are how to win, how to lose, and how to rebound from both.

There Are Also 16 Secondary Traits for Your Success

Athletes in companies are universally respected as high performers, and it is no coincidence that more than 80% of the female executives at Fortune 500 companies described themselves as former athletes. Companies seek employees who can stand out in pressure situations, demonstrate leadership, and react positively to the instruction of superiors. The experience of participating on a competitive team is also a tremendously valuable advantage in the work environment. The understanding of team dynamics and roles, knowing when to step up or when to let someone else step up, and collaboration are also all desired. If you come from team sports, you have already been exposed to workplace dynamics.

> *Here are other valuable traits that highly competitive athletes have been exposed to and most likely possess. Employers are constantly seeking out prospective employees that possess these traits. Check (9) the box beside each characteristic that is strongly descriptive of you.* **Then circle the TOP FIVE characteristics that are your real strengths:**

☐ *Results oriented*

☐ *Focused*

☐ *Handles pressure well*

☐ *Always striving to improve*

- [ ] *Coachable and willing to learn*
- [ ] *Knows how to execute a game plan*
- [ ] *Aggressive or assertive*
- [ ] *Strong work ethic*
- [ ] *Understands importance of preparation*
- [ ] *High energy level*
- [ ] *Strong character*
- [ ] *Self-motivated*
- [ ] *Able to handle multiple tasks simultaneously*
- [ ] *Can make pressure decisions*
- [ ] *Understands accountability*
- [ ] *Seeks and loves a challenge*

Employers Define "Intelligence" in Many Ways

> *To see someone's intelligence, it's important to look at more than just their grades. How do they think? A person can think critically well and draw up thorough conclusions, but their grades could still not be up to par. While this outcome is probably because they are not studying enough (which is stupid unto itself), the fact of the matter is that some athletes just don't test well or work very hard in the classroom.*

In the United States society, intelligence traditionally has been viewed as a kind of general aptitude with which we are born and which cannot be changed much by schooling. In fact, other societies conceptualize intelligence more broadly and view other skills (such as the ability to interact well with others or the ability to create music and art) as valuable and indicative of intelligence.

Howard Gardner, a psychologist at Harvard University, suggested that traditional ways of defining and measuring intelligence with the standard Intelligence Quotient (IQ) test were limiting. He suggested that this traditional conception did a poor job of predicting success in the school context and did not provide much information concerning the person's potential for future growth. In fact, academic success doesn't necessarily translate into successful careers or lives.

Garner conceived eight different types of intelligences and defines intelligence as "the ability to solve problems or make things that are perceived to be valuable in at least one culture." Take a look at these different types of intelligences and see if you can pick one or two that closely matches where you believe your strengths lie:

- ✓ ***Logical and mathematical intelligence.*** Individuals with this type of intelligence generally work easily with numbers and symbols; it is often characteristic of scientists and mathematicians.

- ✓ ***Linguistic intelligence.*** The ability to excel in the use of language, regardless of its form. Writers, poets, journalists, and TV pundits all display the ability to use language to communicate complex thoughts and feelings to help us deal with our world.

- ✓ ***Body and kinesthetic intelligence.*** The ability to control one's body and use it to perform amazing physical feats. Athletes, surgeons, and dancers possess these characteristics.

- ✓ ***Musical intelligence.*** Individuals with musical intelligence actually think in terms of musical themes and progressions.

- ✓ ***Spatial intelligence.*** The ability to understand and see the relationship of objects in a space without borders. Chess, solving puzzles, doing geometry, or even meticulously packing suitcases into the trunk of a car are examples.

- ✓ ***Interpersonal intelligence.*** The ability to truly understand, connect with, and help other people.

- ✓ ***Intrapersonal intelligence.*** Being in touch with one's emotions, feelings, and capacities, being confident of oneself, and being able learn from one's mistakes are characteristics of intrapersonal intelligence. Being at peace with oneself is one of the most valuable goals a person can achieve.

- ✓ ***Naturalist intelligence.*** This is the basic intelligence needed to survive, especially in hostile physical environments. It is ability to understand and negotiate the environments in which a person lives and works.

> *If someone along the way ever questions your intelligence or you feel the need to question someone else's intelligence, try to always remember that intelligence is not always judged by one's GPA or the school we attend. Oftentimes, it is solely judged by the decisions we make in life.*

Chapter 4

Real World Strategies for College Athletes

Start Planning for Your Future Career Today

You are in the best position to look after your interests. As a top athlete, you'll often hear advice from those around you– team owners, parents, coaches, agents, administrators– and the advice is often concentrated 100% on your sport. Sure, if you're in college, there will be equal parts commitment to sports and education, but the underlying advice is to constantly improve yourself so that you are ready and eligible to play and win championships.

Getting an early start on planning your future career is a tough task for many collegiate and elite athletes. Some feel so much pressure that they think they have no time for future career planning. A number of athletes suffer a great deal of anxiety when they begin to think about transitioning from sporting life to their non-competitive athletic lifestyle. So much of their lives has been tied up in being athletes that they have difficulty seeing themselves doing anything else. They know how to get the job done in sports, but many athletes doubt themselves in the new situations they encounter. They don't know if they have what it takes to make it in the business world or their new work career. A number of athletes also have trouble imagining themselves starting a new career in an entry-level job, as if they've somehow forgotten how hard they had to work over the years to reach the level of elite athlete.

Selecting a Major... and a Career

Many students believe that choosing a major is the same as choosing a career. Although this may seem perfectly sensible, it is not always true.

Before you decide on a major, it will be important to give some serious thought to what you want to do five to ten years from now. Perhaps you have had an early working experience in a company or industry or your parents have exposed you to an interesting occupation or calling. If you already have certain career goals in mind today, that's great! This means you can begin to plan pursuits early in your college class selection that will increase your chances of reaching those goals.

> *But having career goals in mind or having no idea what to do next does not mean that you have to make a firm commitment at this point. Having a career goal can help guide the selection of a major, which, in turn, can be a long term goal in and of itself. How important is selecting a major before your junior year? Having a major can help you in the following areas:*

1. Focus.

Having a major provides a built-in way to focus your studies and to make your classes more meaningful, relevant, and coherent. When you have a major, you essentially have an academic game plan. Your major provides the structure for your degree program by identifying the classes you are required to take for graduation and the classes you can select from your degree program. A major can also provide a unifying theme for classes that might appear at first glance to be confusing mix of unrelated areas. Just as your game plan helps you make sense of an individual sequence of plays you run in your sport, having a major can give you a better sense of how your classes fit together. Student-athletes who have developed and declared a major usually have clear goals and are ready to proceed with completing those goals.

2. Connection.

When you have a major, you also have a way of connecting with your college or university. As result, you will have built-in connections with others on campus. Many campus activities and clubs are organized according to the various majors on campus. Your major is your ticket to these valuable experiences, which may also help you with networking as well.

3. Motivation.

Four or five years is a long time to spend taking classes, and almost certainly there will be times when you wonder whether this is worth it. When those times come and you question why you are in school, it will be a big help if you have a major that is meaningful and enjoyable to you. Having a major makes it easy to keep track of your progress toward your degree– and like most students, as a student-athlete, you will feel good about yourself as you complete each requirement of your major.

4. Community Experience.

Another benefit of selecting your major is the opportunity to become active in the local community within areas that serve your major. Many college career centers and athletic departments have established programs that make it easy to serve the community in which the school is located. Some colleges have internships and service learning programs so you can earn course credit for community service. Such activities often provide student-athletes with valuable career development experiences and help them establish networks of contact persons. Many athletes find these experiences to be among the highlights of their collegiate years, as it allows for practical learning lessons that are effectively integrated with their athletic schedules. By taking advantage of these programs, you can have experiences that provide personal and academic rewards while you provide an important service to others.

5. Eligibility.

Finally, as a student-athlete, you need to declare a major in order to maintain your athletic eligibility after certain period of time in school. Many NCAA athletic departments are putting their athletes on a firm track toward academic progress. This means that in order to continue your sports eligibility, you may have to select a major or show that you are making continued progress towards a major and remain on track for graduation.

🎾 A Typical College "Career Prep" Schedule

> *Many athletic departments have outlined what they believe to be an effective road map to graduation for their athletes to pursue while competing in college. While there is no one-way to insure you get exposed to all the important experiences necessary to get out and are ready to go in four years, it does help if you can follow some plan of attack. Here is a four-year planning schedule that I think would fit the bill nicely for any athlete:*

Freshman Year

Major Objective: **Learn how to succeed**

- ✓ Identify interests and explore potential majors
- ✓ Use exercises, projects, psychological tests and other methods to determine your career interests
- ✓ Attend classes and keep your grades as high as you can
- ✓ Investigate internship opportunities
- ✓ Become involved in college other than athletics
- ✓ Explore campus activities and student organizations
- ✓ Attend a career day, career expo, or other career fairs to consider career options and types of jobs available
- ✓ Develop your resume for a summer job
- ✓ Collect, analyze, and evaluate information about yourself to learn about your personality, abilities, attitudes, values, interests, and life experiences
- ✓ Visit the career resource center to learn about the services it provides
- ✓ Find summer work related to your interests to gain work experience and develop a strong work ethic
- ✓ Develop and enhance your ability to interact with people and to function responsibly in a work environment

Sophomore Year

Main Objective: **Explore the possibilities**

- ✓ Discuss career ideas with counselors, friends, faculty, and family
- ✓ Visit the career resource center and attend mini courses on choosing a major

- ✓ Reevaluate your strengths, skills, values, and interests
- ✓ Attend a career expo, career day, and/or other career fairs to talk to company representatives about the qualities and qualifications they seek in employees
- ✓ Join campus organizations and develop leadership skills on and off the playing field
- ✓ Investigate internship opportunities
- ✓ To get a summer job and continue to earn money for expenses. Build a good work reputation and relationships, and acquire work references
- ✓ Gain knowledge about the workplace and what it takes to achieve success
- ✓ Plan, solicit and participate in 2-4 informational interviews

Junior Year

Main Objective: **Establish your career goals**

- ✓ Develop career goals and a strategy plan
- ✓ Develop alternative career plans
- ✓ Reevaluate your strengths, skills, values, and interests
- ✓ Get hands-on experience via an internship, clinical or field experience, or a volunteer position.
- ✓ Attend workshops on resume writing, cover letters, interview skills, job search strategies, and researching occupations and companies
- ✓ Consider graduate school and take the necessary exams
- ✓ Identify companies that interest you
- ✓ Attend career fairs and career day, visiting companies on the list
- ✓ Practice interview skills
- ✓ Network, network, network. Make contact with faculty, counselors, career advisors, administrators, and professionals in your area of interest.
- ✓ Get a summer job in your chosen field
- ✓ Gain more knowledge of the workplace
- ✓ Compile an inventory of interests and qualifications
- ✓ Plan, solicit and participate in 2-4 informational interviews

Senior Year

Main Objective: **It's Showtime… Show me the money!**

- ✓ Reevaluate your strengths, skills, values, and interests

- ✓ Kick your job search campaign into high gear. Commit yourself to a thorough search of interesting companies and opportunities

- ✓ Conduct your own job search, and don't rely on or restrict yourself to campus interviews

- ✓ Discuss career opportunities with faculty, friends, counselors, acquaintances, network contacts, and so on.

- ✓ Attend career fairs to meet employers to set up interviews

- ✓ Develop a career planning log that can be updated with contacts, interview results, and assessments of how you perform during job interviews

- ✓ Register for on-campus interviews and update your resume. Use your network to learn about opportunities for references, and for support

- ✓ Identify and research companies and organizations that interest you and those are actively recruiting job candidates your major

- ✓ Develop a checklist of areas to address when making your transition from college into the work environment

- ✓ Plan, solicit and participate in 2-4 informational interviews

Make Time for Some Experience

Although many college students work in the summer or have part-time jobs during the school year, many student-athletes do not. Why? Simply because it interferes with practice, they don't have the time or because if they worked, their jobs more likely would not be related to their fields of study. For the past several years, school and athletics was your job. So, what's an over programmed, time-strapped student-athlete with little real work experience supposed to do to get real world work experience? The short answer is: Find the time to get a part-time job either in the off-season or during the summer. The long answer is to garner as much practical work experience as you can over the course of your college life.

> *First, it's important to understand what employers are looking for when recruiting for entry-level positions, and that one thing is POTENTIAL! What have you accomplished that demonstrates your potential? Whatever the industry, most entry-level jobs require many of the same qualities and skill sets, including interpersonal skills, problem-solving skills, leadership skills, and the ability to work effectively with others– all skills that the intercollegiate athlete possess in abundance.*

Recruiters also look for involvement in campus activities. I've been told countless times that even with all other things being equal, a recruiter will always offer the job to the student who has been involved in a variety of campus activities over the student who just went back and forth to class for four years. Why? Because being involved suggests the ability to manage one's time more effectively. Being an intercollegiate athlete or holding a position in a club or organization also suggests leadership ability and communication skills and a willingness to stretch yourself.

Most undergraduates have a tendency in college to do very little that will make them look impressive to employers when they graduate. One of the best things you can do to get ready to apply for jobs when you graduate is maintain a good resume. Having a good resume won't land you the job, but it will get your foot in the door and land you an interview. Here are some tips that you might want to consider to spice up your resume:

1. *Create a list of the skills related to your field that you have learned in college.*

Creating a skill set category in your resume in which you list your skills and whether you have a basic, general, or advanced understanding on that topic will help potential employers know what you have learned. If a company is looking for an ASP.NET/C++ programmer and sees "Computer Science Degree" on someone's resume, this doesn't tell the employer whether or not the person actually has any experience in that specific language. So write down your skill set, and be specific. It will help your employers better know who you are.

2. *Take a good inventory of your athletic soft skills or traits.*

You should have your own personal "Top 5" traits that you relate most to as a person and athlete, as well as a corresponding real world example of how each of these traits relate to your potential as an employee. Athletics is one of the most unforgettable and formative experiences individuals can be involved in and, in many ways, is an accurate predictor of future success. Employers know this, and you should be prepared to speak at length about the important work skills you acquired your through competitive athletics experience.

3. *Be involved.*

You can create a "Professional Memberships and Activities" category on your resume to show the potential employer that you are involved. Students who join activities related to their major show employers that the student is well rounded and does more than the bare minimum to get by. Additionally, taking officer positions in these clubs will help demonstrate leadership qualities.

4. *Use your college years to gain experience.*

By participating in some sort of undergraduate research, doing a summer internship, or working part-time in a company related to your field, you are going to show the employer that you are not totally clueless. Doing this will also show the employer you have received some experience in your field while in college and are much more prepared for a private sector job than someone who just went to classes.

5. Get the right references.

Using your neighbor as a reference probably isn't the best option, but you probably know a great number of professors. If those professors know you well enough and believe you would do good work, they would make great references! If you had any experience in your field while in school, be sure to use your previous employers as references too. Those in a particular field will most like know others in their region who operate in the same field and share a common professional respect that may work to your advantage.

6. Visit your career services office.

At most major universities, there will be someone who will take some time to sit down with you, look over your resume, show you some things that you will want to change and improve, and give you ideas to make it more attractive and unique so it stands out in the piles of resumes employers must peruse.

Doing these six things will vastly improve your resume and make you look a lot more attractive to your potential employers. However, you must always remember there is more to life than looking good on paper, so be sure to learn something while you are in school, too. Otherwise, your great new job might not last very long.

The #1 Most Valuable Activity You Can Do!

The Informational Interview

> *As a collegiate athlete, you don't need me to tell you how over-programmed you are and that you have absolutely no extra time for anything. But what if I told you the #1 secret to helping you make the transition from college and sports to a great job took just a little of your free time each semester or quarter? If you're smart, you will find the time for informational interviews throughout your college years.*

One of the easiest and most effective ways to meet people in the professional field you are interested in is to conduct informational interviews. Informational interviewing is a networking approach that allows you to meet many different types of people, gather career information, investigate career options, get advice on job search techniques, and get referrals to other professionals.

Informational interviews also provide a way to explore different careers and discover jobs that have not been advertised to the public. Informational interviewing helps you build your network and gather information. For the most part, the people with whom you conduct informational interviews will not have a job to offer, but they will supply their time, expertise and knowledge of their practice area, and the names of other people for you to contact– and all of this may lead you right into a job offer at some point.

Informal informational interviewing involves setting up an appointment with someone you want to talk to but may not know personally. Because you are an athlete, there are many alumni athletes at your school or former members of your team that would happy to meet with you for an informational interview. Other terrific sources for interviews can be parents of your teammates, contacts from the sports information department (like reporters and editors), and alumni from your desired major who are introduced to you through the Athletic Development Office.

> *An informational interview is one of the few interviews in which you are in control of the questions asked. It is a chance to learn more about a specific career without making a long-term commitment of your time or money. You can find out about the responsibilities, rewards, and problem areas inherent in a specific career by asking questions of people already established in that field.*

When you begin the process of informational interviewing, keep the following things in mind:

- ➢ You are not asking for a job. You are simply asking for information and advice, so you are not putting this person on the spot.

- ➢ You have the right and a responsibility to yourself to seek advice and information from those who can best help you.

- ➢ Because you are interviewing them, you are in charge… and they can relax.

The art of informational interviewing is knowing how to balance your hidden agenda (to expand your network or locate a job) with the unique opportunity to learn firsthand about the demands of various jobs or fields of work. Thus, it is wise to never abuse your privilege by asking for a job in an informational interview; but execute your informational interviews skillfully, and a job may follow.

The primary objectives of informational interviewing are to:

- ✓ Investigate specific careers of interest to you
- ✓ Assist in narrowing your career options
- ✓ Discover employment opportunities that are not advertised
- ✓ Access the most up-to-date career information
- ✓ Determine which skills employers look for in new employees
- ✓ Determine skills to market in your resume or during an interview
- ✓ Help identify your professional strengths and weaknesses

- ✓ Help assess whether your skills are strong enough
- ✓ Obtain advice on where you might fit in
- ✓ Learn the jargon and important issues in the field
- ✓ Broaden your network of contacts for future reference
- ✓ Create a strategy for entering your field of interest
- ✓ Build confidence for your job interviews

How Do You Prepare for Informational Interviews?

You should prepare for your informational interviews just as you would for an actual job interview: polish your presentation and listening skills and conduct preliminary research on the organization. You should outline an agenda that includes some well-thought-out questions.

Begin your interview with questions that demonstrate your genuine interest in the other person: "How did you first get interested in this line of work?" or "Can you describe a typical day in your department?" Then proceed with more general questions: "What are the employment prospects in this field?" or "Are you active in any professional organizations in your field, and which would you recommend?" If appropriate, you can also venture into a series of questions that might open up an advice-giving role: "What should the most important consideration be in my first job?" The whole idea is for you to shine, to make an impression, and to get referrals to other professionals.

> *As a collegiate athlete, it would be best if you targeted two to four informational interviews every year, beginning your sophomore year. That would give you up to 12 separate interviews by the time you are in line for graduation and a great head start on building your network of advisors. If you really hit it off with one of your interviewees, they might even have a job for you after your eligibility expires!*

Final thoughts on informational interviews: you know this already, but always remember to send a thank-you letter to every person who grants you time for an interview and to every individual who refers you to someone. Even though these contacts are not employers who can offer you a job, they will be the most important, influential people you will know in your early career development.

Take Responsibility for Your Career!

If you're reading this, you have probably already learned about self-responsibility and self-motivations, because no one is forcing you to read this chapter. You probably already know what works for you and what keeps your motivation strong through difficult or uncertain times. This means remaining interested in a task or having confidence when others doubt you and not letting others (or laziness) keep you from pursuing something that really interests you or is beneficial.

Athletes who start every game or who play the most minutes are oftentimes the ones who are not as prepared to learn the new skills required for an exceptionally great career. On the other hand, there are also many athletes who are very successful at not only playing their sport, but also taking self responsibility for their career planning and career development. These people not only view themselves as talented athletes, but also as talented people. They have learned to parlay their sports success and life success into a meaningful new personal identity and are ready to compete off the playing field. They do not have tunnel vision and are ready to take self-responsibility!

> *You also have to begin to take responsibility for motivating yourself. Although others can provide some external motivation (like coaches yelling, fans cheering, or red lights flashing in your rear view mirror), external motivators are usually less powerful than internal ones, and their impact tends to diminish when the motivators are no longer present. In turn, motivating yourself has a more lasting impact on your behavior and will lead to even greater persistence, conviction, and self-discipline– all things you will need as you embark on your career path.*

The most effective job search methods require you to take self-responsibility for employment education and your future career. Very simply, what this means is that YOU– and only you– can put the proper priority on learning what it takes to launch and sustain a great career.

Many athletes have never conducted a well-organized job search on their own. Here are some of the new fundamentals that you will need to learn:

- What you want to do
- Where to start
- Whom to contact
- How to dress
- How to best network for job leads
- Which type of resume is best for your situation
- How to write winning resumes and letters
- How to answer and ask questions
- How a behavioral interview differs from a situational interview
- How to ask for the job
- Which follow-up methods work best

As a result of not being prepared to answer to these items, many athletes just stumble into the job market without much focus and make numerous mistakes along the way. It would be like going into a big game without ever having learned the rules of the sport.

The bottom line: Taking self-responsibility for learning effective career planning skills (skills you may not have thought about as important right now) will ultimately help you find careers and jobs that you truly enjoy. Along the way, you may still need to be lucky to land a great job or a rewarding career– but just like in sports, the coach was right when they explained to you that "Luck is when preparation meets opportunity."

Professional Athletes: Special Issues and Considerations

> *Buyer beware! Because you are a highly competitive athlete (either very accomplished at the elite or Division 1 level), you may think you have a future in professional sports. I've seen far too many student-athletes put all their eggs in one basket, so let me say a few words about going pro. Many athletes have dreams of making it all the way to the professional ranks, but only a very small percentage of college student-athletes will ever realize that dream.*

According to the NFL player development program, less than 1% of college football players will make an NFL roster. Less than 1%! And, only 4% played three years or more, with the average career lasting only three and a half years. Likewise, according to the NCAA, only 1.3% of collegiate men's basketball players, 1% of women's basketball players, 4.1% of men's hockey players, and 10.5% of baseball players make it professionally. As discouraging as it might be, you have to face the facts that the odds are not in your favor to go from college to pro.

If you are considering playing professional sports after college, understand your odds. Lying to yourself about those chances will cost monumentally in the long term. You should also know that the average career is short lived, and most professional athletes retire in their twenties; in other words, they leave the game at least thirty-five years before retirement age.

The question is not if you will have to do something after your sports career, but when, what, and for how long. What will you be prepared to do? You are used to having a Plan B if your strategy is not working in a game, so you should also have a Plan B in case your dreams of becoming a professional athlete don't pan out– or end all too soon.

It's very difficult making your first career decisions at twenty-eight to thirty-two, and in some cases as late as thirty-five years old. Why? The longer you exist in your sports-only realm, the more the world around you will change and the more foreign it will become to you. It would be like stumbling into a Latin class when all you're really capable of doing in texting on your phone. But at some point, every athlete has to make the transition from playing professional sports to doing something else. In my experience, there are two types of professional or elite athletes: those who plan for this transition ahead of time and those who don't. The ones who plan ahead typically experience less of an emotional roller coaster and find more fulfilling roles than those who don't. Even if you have plenty of money saved up for retirement, you will still have decades of productive life left in you to contribute, experience new challenges, and continue to make your dreams come true.

Professional athletes like to think of themselves as entertainers, but there's a far shorter peak earnings window than in any other profession, and in many cases, athletes lack the time and desire to understand and monitor their investments. More often than not, the money you earn as a professional athlete will disappear quickly... sometimes through a misplaced trust in shady agents and unscrupulous financial advisors, a 60 to 80% divorce rate for professional athletes, a huge posse and bling, or a Wall Street meltdown (just for good measure). Statistically, you have a few very good reasons that you better have plans for a career after you're finished playing professional sports.

The good news is that professional athletes' salaries have risen steadily in the last three decades. The bad news is, sadly, that by the time NFL players have been retired two years, 78% of them have either gone bankrupt or are under financial stress because of joblessness or divorce. In a less public way, other athletes from the nation's three biggest and most profitable leagues (the NBA, NFL, and MLB) are suffering from a financial pandemic. A host of sources (athletes, players associations, agents and financial advisors) indicate that within five years of retirement, an estimated 60% of former NBA players are broke. Similarly, numerous retired MLB players have been similarly ruined, and the current economic crisis is taking a toll on some active athletes as well.

If all that's not enough, the online reseller www.championship-rings.net reports that over 400 championship title rings have been pawned over one recent three-month period, including a 2008 Giants Super Bowl ring! Throw in the bankruptcies and near financial ruin of Hall-of-Famers Kareem Abdul-Jabbar, Tony Gwynn, John Unitas, and Brooks Robinson, and money troubles abound for professional athletes old and new.

> *If you are currently an elite or professional athlete, it's time to begin thinking about your career after your last game. Here are six keys to planning for your career transition proactively:*

1. Prepare mentally for the transition.

The transition from the prestige and status of being a professional athlete to becoming a "regular person" is not always easy. Many athletes face a period of depression and grieving. Some make reckless decisions and get into trouble. Others find that they haven't saved enough money to keep up with their spending and get into financial trouble. EVERY athlete needs to be thinking about the inevitable transition with a realistic, positive, proactive attitude.

2. Leverage your relationships.

Professional athletes have rare VIP access to wealthy, powerful, and connected people. Now is the time to build your network– while you still have your status as an elite athlete. That way, doors will open for you long after your playing days end.

3. What are your dreams?

Despite what you may believe, playing golf and sitting by the pool every day gets boring in about six months. You have lots of time left to fulfill new dreams if you take time to think about your passions, ambitions, and aspirations. What would be something you could do after sports that would get you excited to wake up every day and contribute?

4. Assess yourself and know who you are as the "product."

We all have different talents, values, and personality styles. Some athletes will make superb coaches or general managers, while many will not. Some will be natural entrepreneurs. Others will be leaders in the public sector or a nonprofit foundation. Many will be excellent salespeople or leaders in large companies. You need to invest some time to think about who you are, what you can offer, and what kinds of skills you want to develop to achieve your dreams.

5. What does the market have to say?

Eventually, your dreams and talents need to find a niche in the marketplace. It is important for you to do some research now. For instance, many athletes want to start a restaurant chain with their name on the door. However, given that most restaurants fail within a year, these would-be entrepreneurs should research to learn what it really takes to run a successful restaurant and how they can attract the resources and talent who can make the restaurant thrive. Regardless of your aspirations, you need to be talking to people and doing some homework to learn about the requirements of the marketplace.

6. Create a transition development plan.

Once you know what you want to do and what it will take to succeed, you can create a plan to be ready for your transition. What skills will you need to learn? Who are people you know who can help you? What is the action plan to succeed?

7. Get a career coach.

While I may have mentioned this many times before, it is a very important step. Investing in your career is one of the smartest things you can do financially. Getting a good grasp of your skill set, knowing the value can bring to an organization, and possessing the ability to communicate why you would be the best candidate to hire is a challenge for any athlete. It is especially challenging for a former professional athlete that has been away from the working world for some time. Hiring a good career coach is a necessity and requirement. If you want to discuss whether or not a career coach is right for you, contact me through my website at *www.careerball.net* and I'll be happy to talk through your options.

Chapter 5

Assessing Your Personal Interests

I know of an exceptional athlete who was the starting center on his D1 basketball team and made the decision to give up his final year of college eligibility. When he broke this news to the press, he said:

> *"It's physically and emotionally time to pursue other things. I'm on pace to complete my degree this spring, and I've played basketball long enough. I love the game, but it's not my entire life. I'm just curious to see what other challenges are out there away from the court."*

This kid had a pretty good idea of who he was and what he wanted in life. Do you?

⚾ *Finding the Right Fit*

Finding the right job comes down to just one thing: keeping it simple. By simplifying the process, it's easier to achieve success. Most people feel finding the right job can be a very intimidating process. For this reason, many job hunters have difficulty getting started because they don't know where to begin. Rather than being focused on accurately assessing themselves, they end up settling for the first job that comes along.

Most people don't know how to take a compliment, let alone talk about their achievements in a job interview. It can be difficult to sell yourself to employers, especially if you haven't really taken the time to uncover your true assets.

Your goal should be to get really clear on who you are as an individual and what you offer your current and potential employers. Just like a diamond in the rough, you need to chip away and find your most brilliant center. Then, you need to spend some time polishing it so that it really shines.

> *Invest the extra time and effort now to eliminate jobs that are not a good fit for you, and you'll actually spend less time on your job and career development. It's kind of like a carpenter's advice: "Measure twice... cut once." What you devote to this all-important first step of your job search is directly proportionate to the amount of success you will achieve. It's that simple.*

Understanding what you want out of life can help you to make trade-offs when it comes to your job. Knowing your personality, work value, work interests, and athlete core message is more than most job seekers ever take the time to figure out. Accumulating this information and assessing it can tell you a lot about what you value in a career and in life– and how to avoid a lifetime of disappointment and poor job satisfaction.

First Up: Assess Yourself

The first step in career planning involves gathering information about yourself in order to make a wise decision about a career. Assessing yourself is a lifelong process. Your goals may change as you learn more about yourself and your values, needs, objectives, and other areas of interest. This initial focus will help you narrow your options and target appropriate employers.

> *Each and every one of us has our own individual, unique set of skills, talents, and ambitions. Identifying one's skills and talents is essential to your success. A skill is something you've learned to do, while a talent is something you've been born with, or at least that you seem naturally qualified to do. Recognizing the difference between the two is an important step in assessing yourself.*

You may be skilled at something and still not find it interesting. Chances are, however, if you are naturally talented at something, there will be a corresponding link between that particular talent and your interests. Put another way, you are more apt to enjoy doing what you do well naturally than what you have simply been taught to do.

Besides knowing what you want at various times of your life, when it comes to your career, knowing what you do well– your skills, abilities, and aptitudes– is essential for making good decisions. But it is no easy task to accurately identify your own strengths and find jobs that specifically match your strengths and capabilities. In the career world, your "qualifications" will consist of your skills, abilities, and aptitudes; and these are important for focusing your job search and communicating your strengths to prospective employers.

Career planning and goal setting is something that you need to do on a continuous basis, because your qualifications and interests change over time. What helps the most in career planning is to really understand your skills, abilities, and talents, because when these things are clear in your head, career planning is much more productive.

It is important that you set goals in your career-planning efforts. Without goals and targets, you are likely going to be lost and confused. Realistic goals are important. It is simply not beneficial to set goals that are unrealistic and unachievable. The key here is to realize that when you set realistic goals and achieve them, you will feel good about yourself and work doubly hard at your career.

Put yourself into the mind frame of having just won $30 million in the lottery. All the pressure is off, and you don't need to work– not for another day in your life! But, rather than do absolutely nothing, for the first time in your life, you're now in the position to do something that's personally satisfying rather than financially rewarding. This attitude forces you to place more importance on personally satisfying issues rather than financial significance alone.

With work, chances are the money will probably be the same in either a job you mostly like or one you mostly dislike. The difference is, people who are passionate about what they do achieve far greater success in their work life in the form of bonuses, raises, and promotions.

In your sport, it is important to find a position that best suits your talents. In your career, you ultimately want to find the occupation and work setting that fits you best so you can maximize your chances of career success and satisfaction. The better the fit, the more satisfied you will be, and the longer and better you are likely to work in your chosen career. A poor fit creates unhappy workers and employers.

> *The best way to optimize your fit is to know these three important factors about yourself:*
>
> 1. *What is your personality style? How do you typically interact with others and with the environment?*
> 2. *What are your work values? What is important to you?*
> 3. *What are your work interests? What do you like to do?*

Essential to job and career satisfaction is matching your own unique talents, skills, interests, and personality to those job-related tasks and activities you find most enjoyable, interesting, and challenging. By performing this self analysis, you'll have the opportunity (perhaps for the first time in your career) to choose the position and organization that is personally satisfying as well as financially rewarding.

Do Personality Tests Work?

There is something very appealing, almost magical, about taking computerized and/or pencil and paper psychological, career planning, and guidance tests and inventories that are designed to simplify reality. For some people, these tests are potentially the magic bullet to discovering what they should do with the rest of their life. While no such bullet exists, these self-focused devices can nevertheless be very useful at the initial stage of one's job search.

If all goes well, an analysis will provide you a general picture or outline of who you really are in terms of your personality, interests, skills, abilities, attitudes, and temperaments, as well as evidence of where you may be going in the future.

Most of these comprehensive career planning programs do much more than just assess skills; they also integrate other key components in the career planning process such as interests, goals, related jobs, college majors, education and training programs, and job search plans. These programs are widely available in schools, colleges, and libraries across the country. You might check with your career counseling centers to see what computerized career assessment systems are available for your use. Relatively easy to use, they generate a great deal of useful first-step career planning information, and many will provide you with a print out of your personal analysis and how your interests and skills are related to specific jobs and careers.

⑨ Indentifying Your Work Personality is Important

It is your personality style that largely defines the ways in which you interact with your environment and other people. Unfortunately, personality factors are often overlooked by students during the process of choosing a major and a career. This oversight is a problem, because one of the main causes of dissatisfaction with a career choice is the poor fit between an individual's personality and the demands of the job in the work environment. As a result, it is important to carefully assess your own personality before you make a choice, as certain jobs and occupations also have personalities of their own.

> *Ideally, you would want to try to match your work personality closely with your own personality. There are six basic types of individual personalities, as we've discussed earlier. Now, let's review those types to see where you fall. Take a close look at the following, and check (9) the box beside each personality that is strongly descriptive of you.* **Then circle the TOP THREE values that really fit you.**

☐ *Realistic.*

The realistic type places the greatest emphasis on working with objects. Realistic types like to work with their hands in jobs that require the use of machinery, tools, and equipment. They are active in life and problem solving. Examples of realistic occupations include engineer, airplane pilot, mechanic, web programmer, and construction worker.

☐ *Investigative.*

The investigative type places the greatest emphasis on working with data and ideas. Investigative types may appear reserved or introverted. They are typically strong in mathematics and the sciences and enjoy intellectual pursuits and solving problems by thinking them through. Investigative occupations include chemist, pharmacist, physician, and sociologist.

☐ *Artistic.*

The artistic type may emphasize working with ideas or objects, depending upon this person's preferred mode of expression. Artistic types focus on beauty, form, sound, color, and aesthetics, and may sometimes seem unorganized or unfocused. They enjoy solving problems through creating and viewing situations in novel ways. Examples of artistic occupations are architect, clothing designer, writer, musician, actor, painter and photographer.

☐ *Social.*

The social type places the greatest emphasis on working with people. Many athletes are primarily social. They enjoy relationships, like to work with people individually or in groups, and often assume roles involving teaching and leadership. They typically have good social skills, but they lack scientifically mechanical interests and abilities. They approach solving problems by involving others. Examples of social occupations include athletic trainer, coach, professional athlete, clinical psychologist, teacher, physical therapist, and social worker.

☐ Enterprising.

The enterprising type also places the greatest emphasis on working with people, although differently than the social types. Enterprising types like to work with people by managing, selling, directing, and achieving. They enjoy status, power, and money, and solve problems by taking risks and try new things. Enterprising occupations include manager, business owner or entrepreneur, lawyer, sales representative, and broadcaster.

☐ Conventional.

The conventional personality type places emphasis on working with objects, data, and people. Conventional types like to work in environments where order and control are valued and they generally possess clerical, analytic, and organizational skills. They excel with details and solve problems by following rules and established procedures. Examples of this type include accountant, building inspector, financial analysts, clerical worker, and bookkeeper.

Although presented independently here, these six personality types are integrally related to one another and share common features, but to varying degrees. In fact, most people are not just one particular type of personality (such as social or artistic), but are best described by a combination of two or three of these types. What elements of each personality do you most closely relate to? Determining this can be a key factor to finding a job in which you will thrive.

🏆 Ranking Your Work Values

What is important to you, what matters to you, and what you care about are your values. They define your everyday perspective, attitudes, motivations, and your whole way of life– including whom you want to associate with on a daily basis. For example, people who identify with a certain political party or religion have values that line up with that specific group of people and will often go to great lengths to promote and protect the groups shared values.

> *Understanding your values is essential to success, be it athletic, academic, or personal, because your values provide meaning and direction in life. They can promote reflection and action and bring about strong emotions. If you're unclear as to your values, you are like a ship without a rudder. You will likely be in motion, but without a clear direction or sense of purpose.*

Everyone lives by a specific set of values. Some are more important than others. We will sacrifice a lower value for one we consider to be more important. Obviously, to have a career you love, you want one that reflects your values. For some people, their careers need to be entirely about furthering some value. For others, it is enough that the career does not conflict with the values. Because one's values generally develop through personal experiences and family influences, they are likely to vary from person to person.

Signs of your values are everywhere: who you hang out with, what stuff you have, how you spend your time and money, how you react to people, and what attracts you to someone or someplace have all been shaped by your values. For example, if you value being creative, you probably do things that involve creating something new or unusual. If you value challenging the status quo, some of your best friends might embody that attitude. If being secure is very important you, chances are that you don't take very many risks. If social status and looking good to others is one of your values, you will find it necessary to own some material things like a car, clothes, gadget club memberships, and friends that will not hesitate to freely announce your status to the world around you. At every moment throughout your life, much of who you are has been sculpted by your values.

Work values are those things you like to do– the things that give you true pleasure and enjoyment. Most jobs involve a combination of likes and dislikes. Identifying what you both like and dislike about jobs or how closely you can match a job to your own personal work values will help you better identify jobs that involve tasks that you will most enjoy doing.

> *Take a close look at the following work values. Check (9) the box beside each personality that is strongly descriptive of you.* ***Then circle the TOP FIVE values that really fit you.***

☐ *Adventure:* working in a job that requires taking risks.

☐ *Authority:* working in a job in which you use your position to control others.

☐ *Competition:* working in a job in which you compete with others.

☐ *Creativity and Self-Expression:* working in a job in which you use your imagination to find new ways to do or say something.

☐ *Flexible Work Schedule:* working in a job in which you choose your hours to work.

☐ *Helping Others:* working in a job in which you provide direct services to persons with problems.

☐ *High Salary:* working in a job where many workers earn a large amount of money.

☐ *Independence:* working in a job in which you decide for yourself what to do and how to do it.

- [ ] **Influencing Others:** working in a job in which you influence the opinions of others or decisions of others.

- [ ] **Intellectual Stimulation:** working in a job that requires a great amount of thought and reasoning.

- [ ] **Leadership:** working in a job in which you direct, manage, or supervise the activities of other people.

- [ ] **Outside Work:** working outdoors.

- [ ] **Persuading:** working in a job in which you personally convince others to take certain actions.

- [ ] **Physical Work:** working in a job that requires substantial physical activity.

- [ ] **Prestige:** working in a job that gives you status and respect in the community.

- [ ] **Public Attention:** working in a job in which you attract immediate notice because of appearance or activity.

- [ ] **Public Contact:** working in a job in which you deal directly with the public on a daily basis.

- [ ] **Recognition:** working in a job in which you gain public notice.

- [ ] **Research Work:** working in a job in which you search for and discover new facts and develop ways to apply them.

- [ ] **Routine Work:** working in a job in which you follow established procedures requiring little change.

- [ ] **Seasonal Work:** working in a job in which you are employed only at certain times of the year.

- [ ] **Travel:** working in a job in which you take frequent trips.

- [ ] **Variety:** working in a job in which your duties change frequently.

- [ ] **Work with Children:** working a job in which you teach or care for children.

- [ ] **Work with Your Hands:** working in a job in which you use your hands or hand tools.

☐ **Work with Machines or Equipment:** working in a job where you utilize machines or equipment.

☐ **Work with Numbers:** working in a job in which you use mathematics or statistics.

Matching Your Work Interests

We all have interests, and most of them change over time. Many of your interests may be centered on your sports participation, school or present job; whereas others relate to activities that define your hobbies and leisure activities; and still others may relate to your dreams and aspirations.

Knowing what you want from a job is critical in your job search, saving you time and giving you an edge during interviews. Understanding this important part of your career profile will allow you to sell yourself to employers as the right person for the right job.

Before you start your career planning and goal setting, you need to have some sense of what's inside of you. You need to understand what interests you have and what matters the most. Initially, it is easiest to just ask yourself two important questions and see if you can answer them. These questions will help you enormously with your lifetime career planning:

1. What are you passionate about?
2. What would you like to do every day?

> *Take a close look at the following work values.* ***Rank these areas or work interest from 1 (most interesting) to 12 (least interesting).*** *Identifying and understanding your TOP FIVE work interests– the ones that really fit you– is critical to enjoying a meaningful, rewarding, and satisfying job career.*

_____ **Administration**

Enjoys organizing the financial or day-to-day operations of a business or institution, supervising the activities of others, planning work schedules, and maintaining records.

_____ **Art**

Has a special appreciation for the arts and enjoys participation in them. This may involve performing on stage or creating visual artwork.

_____ **Clerical**

Enjoys office work of a systematic nature, involving attending to details and routine duties.

_____ **Food Service**

Likes to be involved in the preparation, serving, or selling of food products.

_____ **Industrial Art**

Enjoys making or repairing things using machinery or by hand.

_____ **Health Service**

Interested in helping to prevent, diagnose, or cure diseases through laboratory work or by attending to the health needs of individuals directly.

_____ **Humanitarian**

Interested in helping others with their mental, spiritual, social, physical, or vocational needs.

_____ **Outdoors**

Likes working outdoors, especially in agriculture with animals and/or plants. May enjoy the challenge of potentially dangerous situations.

_____ **Personal Service**

Likes interacting with others and providing the public with services involving personal contact.

_____ **Sales**

Interested in selling merchandise or services. This usually involves an understanding of products and services, informing customers of their features, demonstration, and being persuasive with others.

_____ **Science**

Enjoys working with abstract ideas, scientific equipment, and mathematical logic and reasoning to solve practical or abstract problems.

_____ **Teaching/Social Service**

Enjoys instructing people in learning new things, helping people solve problems, and assisting others.

_____ **Writing**

Enjoys either creative or technical writing. Likely to have broad interests. 7

_____ **Assertive**

Prefers working in situations in which it is appropriate to assert authority over others and to direct and monitor their work.

_____ **Persuasive**

Enjoys work which involves influencing, advising, counseling, guiding, motivating, or directing the activities of others.

_____ **Systematic**

Prefers jobs that involve routine but challenging assignments in which order and persistent, steady effort are required. Likes job security to be established, and dislikes frequent changes in schedule and situations requiring quick decisions.

The difference between getting a job and discovering what you love to do is the work required to fully understand your own personality, your work values, and your work interests. Take note of your personal assessment, for you will need to know these things about yourself to perform a successful job hunt that leads to job satisfaction.

Job Satisfaction is Very Important

> *Evidence has shown that job satisfaction can profoundly affect one's personal quality of life. Positive attributes such as emotional stability, security, optimism, and happiness can play a significant role in achieving one's goals. Finding rewarding and satisfying work can even prevent illness and disease by helping an individual maintain a healthier immune system. The bottom line is, let's work hard to get you in the right job and right career where you'll be gaining more than just a paycheck!*

Every job you have ever had, even in athletics, required some tasks you enjoyed and some you dreaded. Not surprisingly, people tend to perform more effectively when their job tasks and responsibilities correspond with their personal or career interests. How much satisfaction you derive from work is directly linked to the match-up between your personal career interests and the scope of a specific job.

Even if your work fits your personality, values and interests, it isn't going to be satisfying unless you are truly interested in the work you do. For some people, it is enough that the subject matter is interesting or that the talents, functions, and environment fit. But many people want to do something they consider meaningful or make a contribution to other people or the world around them.

Think about what you enjoy doing, what is important to you, and what you do well. Ask yourself these questions:

➢ What activities do you engage in that bring you the most satisfaction?

➢ What kinds of activities do others ask you to perform?

➢ Were you ever acknowledged, presented with an award, or praised for something you did?

- What skills and talents have you used in the past to achieve goals?
- Were you ever told you do certain things better than others?
- Think of a time when you felt successful. What were you doing?
- What motivates you to jump out of bed in the morning raring to go?
- Was there ever a time that you achieved results that exceeded your/others expectations?
- Was there something you did that made you feel proud?

Now, ask those very same questions and try not to use any sports-related examples. If you can't, then you should really think strongly about a career in the field of sports such as coaching, athletic administration, sports agency, etc, or consider spending some quality time exploring your non-athletic interests. If you still have problems coming up with a non-sports list, then you may be one of those "tunnel vision" athletes we spoke about earlier.

Remember… understanding the value of the strengths and accomplishments you have gained gives you an edge during interviews by helping you answer the question, "Why should I hire you?" Do you know what kind of career would make you happy? If yes, what are you doing now to prepare yourself? How committed are you to achieving your own career happiness?

What is Your Individual Athlete Trait Profile?

> *Let's go back and see which athlete traits you circled as your real strengths (pages 38-41). Take the top three you circled from the ten primary athlete skills and the top five you circled from the sixteen secondary reasons for your success. Every athlete will have their own mix of traits, and each athlete is defined by their own experiences.*

Top Three Primary Traits you possess:

1. _____

2. _____

3. _____

Top Five Secondary Traits you possess:

1. _____

2. _____

3. _____

4. _____

5. _____

Now, take a minute and think back through your many competitive athletic experiences and identify an event (practice, game, tournament) or a person (teammate, coach, competitor) or a circumstance (decision, outcome or missed opportunity) that you can associate with each of your real strengths. These examples will become your Athlete Trait Profile that you will use throughout your career.

> *Here is an example of how you can use your Individual Athlete Trait Profile in job interviews if you need to overcome a lack of tangible work experience, a lack of work content skills, or simply need communicate to perspective employers that you have the necessary qualifications to be successful as a valuable employee.*

Sample Profile Trait:

1. Ability to organize time well

Example:

"I spend thirty hours a week in my sport; complete a full academic load; find three hours a night to get everything done; prioritize all my academic, social, and athletic requirements; and juggle multiple tasks to get it all done."

How it can relate to your employer/career:

"When organizations reorganize or downsize or cut the budget, employees have to do their work and then some. Organizations like to have employees who can handle multiple tasks and manage time effectively– someone who can say, 'I can self-manage my tasks and responsibilities without the constant oversight of my supervisor'."

Now, take each of your Top Eight Athlete Profile Traits (the ones you just listed above) and write a brief example of what you have learned from your athletic participation, and then think about how it can relate to your employer or career. The idea is to capture real-life examples demonstrating how your personal traits are instrumental in satisfying the demands of your everyday life and how those will help you in your career.

🎾 *Your Individual Athlete Core Message*

> *Every highly competitive athlete should have an Individual Athlete Core Message. Your core message is your overall plan for what you will say about your athletic experience in your job search and how you will say it. It needs to be honest, carefully planned, and completely positive. It should focus on the needs of the decision-makers in the kind of organization you've targeted and on what you have to offer them, covering all of the important selling points that you have acquired as a competitive athlete.*

The key to a successful Individual Athlete Core Message is focusing on the group of jobs that have been refined by assessing your personality, work vales, and interests; and then, most importantly, overlaying the athlete traits you identified. Do not forget the valuable soft skills you have acquired through a lifetime of competitive athletics.

Even if you've never held any job in interest areas that you have identified as a "fit," your athlete core message is intended to provide evidence that you can do that kind of work. You should mention skills, experience, abilities, personality, knowledge, competence, education, athlete traits, and other personal characteristics you possess that are relevant to the particular group of jobs you seek. Convincing people that you can do that kind of work well is the objective of your athlete core message.

Often, the most convincing evidence of your effectiveness is a story about a past success in similar work or athletic experience. These are everyday performance stories of how you went the extra mile in something, experienced adversity of a particular situation and bounced back, or personally became involved with a trying situation and helped the team achieve a positive result. Oftentimes, these stories illustrate your athlete traits and soft skills.

It's your job throughout your job search to tell the decision-makers how effective you will be in the job. As an integral part of your Individual Athlete Core Message, you should have at least five "go-to stories" that support your capabilities and demonstrate your accomplishments. For example, they might highlight the most satisfying moments you experienced as an athlete and what you learned from the experience, or how you improved moral of a teammate, helped your coach achieve an important objective, or increased your personal or team productivity through acts or deeds you initiated. These stories should be centered on the skills you possess that might not readily appear in a resume or cover letter. And don't forget that in spite of how excited you might get when you remember these stories, they should always be told in one or two minutes.

> *Your core message can also be summarized as a two-minute verbal statement crafted to convince decision-makers how unique you are or that you can do the work outlined in the job description. Your Individual Athlete Core Message consists of your most relevant experience, skills, education, training, and credentials. If you are asked to outline yourself in written format, these one or two-minute stories may also appear as a four to six-line summary statement. The verbal version can be used with everyone you talk to throughout your search process– prospective employers, mentors, on informational interviews and when attending job fairs on campus.*

You should practice using your Individual Athlete Core Message in conversation in a relaxed way so it doesn't sound "canned." And don't worry too much about self-promotion. I believe there are two reasons why people understate their value. First, in normal conversations, modesty is a virtue. While people are sometimes justifiably proud of their work, most don't brag. Second, most young adults have gotten better at doing certain kinds work or acquired transferable skills without realizing it. Many athletes have not prepared a list of their top athlete traits and the soft skills they have acquired, and they may not have a way of gauging the strength of those experiences and skills. You do! This means that it's important for you to label and be able to describe your skills and traits. It may first feel like you're bragging when you describe them, but you need to create your Individual Athlete Core Message so that it honestly tells everyone what you have to offer.

Chapter 6

The Power of the Mentor

The term "mentor" is seductive. To many, it is assumed that having a mentor is the magic key to finding a job and securing lifelong career success. Many bigger athletic departments provide formal and informal mentoring programs that incorporate a strong network of coaches, academic advisors, administrators, and alumni athlete organizations– all committed to providing a support system for current student-athletes. Many professional sports leagues and player associations also provide access to former athletes and individuals that can assist you in making the transition to a work career that much easier.

> *When you have completed competitive athletics, it is of paramount importance that all former athletes consider developing a strong career mentor relationship to help guide them through this difficult transition. A job mentor serves as a catalyst and a partner, providing support in your job search and guiding you toward professional success and fulfillment. Mentors can offer a fresh perspective on seemingly daunting issues and can provide creative but proven career advice for handling the challenges you may face in your career and your life.*

A good mentoring relationship is reciprocal. Because mentoring is a two-way street, it's important to understand what's involved. There is a mutual time commitment, a shared emotional investment in each other, and the creation of a trust and bond between two individuals. Meaningful mentoring relationships are difficult to develop, delicate to manage, and change over time as the partners learn to communicate with each other.

Of course, mentoring is not a new concept. The original Mentor can he traced to Greek mythology. Today, mentoring is an accepted process that links an experienced individual with someone who needs support and guidance. A good mentor relationship can help almost every young person who is just starting out in their career and can facilitate career development and expand opportunities for those who are traditionally hindered by organizational barriers (such as women and minorities). Today, many organizations are using formal mentoring programs, often geared specifically to women and minorities as a way of helping them break into the "Good 'Ol Boy Network" and burst through the seemingly impenetrable glass ceiling.

For many athletes, their coach in later life (who they developed the most respect for and successfully opened a communication dialog with) is the most likely mentor they seek out. The problem with an athletic coach as an advisor for your career is that oftentimes coaches come directly from academia or sports themselves and possess no "real world" experiences. Compounding the problem, coaches in today's highly competitive landscape often lack skills and time to effectively mentor the growing legions of former athletes that seek their attention.

🍀 Characteristics of a Good Mentor

Everyone should strive to have a good mentor on their side. Having a good mentor relationship established from the moment you complete your athletic career can prove to be invaluable. A good mentor can help you set and achieve your goals, avoid career mistakes, help you establish your network, navigate office politics, or assist you in correctly reading career signals that periodically pop up.

Here a few tips on finding a mentor who can help you grow and develop as young professional:

1. A mentor should have experience in the field in which you work, or aspire to work.

    Obviously, a mentor who is experienced in your chosen field is going to be able to assist you with more knowledge and expertise. A mentor should work in your type of field or profession. For example, if you are an accountant or aspiring accountant, you should choose an experienced senior-level accountant to mentor you. New auditors or future auditors should find an experienced auditor to mentor them, and so on.

2. Choose a mentor who is local or nearby, if possible, and ideally someone in your organization.

    Not only is it more convenient to have your mentor nearby, it also enables your mentor to guide you through situations that may be specific to your area such as economical, political, or legal issues which may affect your role. For example, some jobs, duties, authority, and autonomy vary from state to state for many companies. Additionally, laws and licensing requirements for each state may be different, and local experience can really help.

3. Find a mentor who has a good balance of similarities and differences compared to your strengths and weaknesses.

    If you select a mentor who is a total opposite of yourself, you may find that it's too difficult for you to relate to that person. Therefore, it could be challenging to follow their lead and guidance. On the other hand, if you choose a mentor who is exactly like you in every way, he or she may not be able to add as much to your existing skill set as someone whose strengths balance out your weak areas to help you grow. Ideally, you should try to find an individual who shares your values, work style, and sense of humor. If you can locate a former competitive athlete that understands the value of your acquired soft skills, this would be an ideal candidate.

4. Finding a mentor doesn't have to be a formal arrangement.

    You don't have to declare someone your mentor, or have them sign an agreement. A mentor can be someone who is a friend or coworker who happens to be in a professional position which lends itself to being your mentor. If the person is willing to answer questions, give advice, and lend a helping hand from time to time, you have yourself a mentor! That being said, a mentor should definitely be a willing participant. If you are not sure, you may certainly ask your prospective mentor by saying something such as, "Your career has been very successful, and I think I could learn a great deal from your experience. Would you mind if turn to you as a mentor and resource for answers to career-related questions or for problem-solving advice?"

The Right Mentor Can Help Develop Your Career

Once you find the best mentor who is in the right professional role and who has the right characteristics, here are a few ways a mentor may be able to assist you in developing and advancing your career for optimum success:

> *Networking contacts.* An experienced mentor will have accrued and collected a number of professional contacts in the field, which could soon become your professional networking contacts!

> *Navigate politics and bureaucracy.* Job titles tell you who has authority at any given organization, but a mentor can tell you who has the power. Politics are a part of any organization, and missteps can be costly. A mentor can also help promote you within the organization to key players who can help advance your career.

> *Learn what they did not teach you in school.* You have learned many theories, principles, and formulas. You may have even worked as an intern or be familiar with a profession. But now that you're working at a job for real, there are many situations you will encounter that were not taught in school. A mentor can help fill in the blanks between theoretical knowledge and practical know-how.

Make Your Relationship with Your Mentor Meaningful

A good mentor is knowledgeable, generous, a good communicator, and committed to the relationship. You may be lucky enough to have someone such as this already in your life. However, in most cases, you'll need to recruit one. Here are some tips for finding a career mentor, soliciting their support, and making it a meaningful relationship.

Step 1: Develop a short list of folks who can potentially help.

Identify one or two folks in each of the following categories:

- Peers – friends, relatives, current/former teammates who are pursuing similar tracks and ideally are a little ahead of you

- Job/recruiting contacts – folks you have met through your job search activities to date who work at organizations that you are pursuing

- Experienced professionals – friends of friends/family, alumni of your schools, former bosses who have connections, opportunities and wisdom

Step 2: Make smart requests that are easy for them to respond with "yes."

- Smart requests are ones that are in your contact's "sweet spot" in terms of their ability to help you and are consistent with how well they know you.

- First, share the opportunities you are pursuing, initially by offering to send them your resume and a sample cover email for a target job. You may want to include three or four bullet points that best describe how you communicate

- Your key selling points and ask them for feedback. Second, you will want them to know how important your goal is to developing an effective mentor relationship and how you think you can benefit from this relationship.

Step 3: Make it easy for them to help you.

Your follow-up requests should be as little work for your mentor as possible. Here are four requests in ascending order of the amount of work required for them:

- "Can I say in my note that you recommended that I reach out?" (no work for them other than providing the contact information)

- "Would you be willing to send the contact a heads-up email that I plan to reach out to them?" (moderate amount of work)

- "Would you be willing to do a quick email introduction for the two of us?" (moderate amount of work)

- "Would you write or call on my behalf recommending they speak with me?" (potentially a significant amount of work). If they say "yes," then offer to give them a few bullet points to include in their note on what you are seeking to do and why you are a compelling person/candidate.

Step 4: Asking for Their Support.

- Before you ask for support, prepare a plan. What exactly do you expect of them? If you're asking this person to commit, they need to know what they are getting into. It is not reasonable to ask for more than one meeting a month. Define the type of guidance you need. For example, you may want to present yourself on an interview a certain way and want help creating an action plan. Be as specific as you can.

♦ Invite the potential mentor to meet to discuss your career. Assure them that you are not asking for a job– you're just looking for some advice and counsel. At the meeting, define the relationship and your vision. Most importantly, don't assume the person you are asking will say "yes." If you sense they are not sure, ask them to think about it overnight. Give them room to say "no." If they feel pressured to accept, you may not get the level of participation you want.

♦ If you are already employed, you should not expect your current boss to become your mentor. It is very unique for your manager to also be your mentor because it is very difficult for this person to be objective on issues of job performance, office politics, or advancement. Look for senior people within your company who have been along a career path similar to yours. Also look beyond your company to company partners, affiliates, and related companies. Professional associations are a good way to meet top people in your field.

Questions to Ask Your Mentor

Here are some of my favorite questions to ask your mentor. You may develop other that fit your particular circumstances, but once you get the conversation rolling, you will have no trouble finding important topics to explore and discuss together.

Obtaining Employment & Advancement

✓ What are the most important skills someone should possess to achieve success in this occupation?

✓ What types of part-time, full-time or summer jobs should I be doing right now which may prepare me for this career path?

✓ What avenues did you explore to find job openings in your field?

✓ What kind of experience is needed to obtain an entry-level position in this profession?

✓ How long should I expect to stay in an entry-level position?

✓ What are the opportunities for advancement?

✓ Is this type of work available on an international basis (without further training)?

Education

- ✓ In what ways did your education contribute to your career?
- ✓ What academic courses do you find most relevant to your day-to-day work?
- ✓ Is a post-graduate certificate or diploma necessary within this field?

Networking

- ✓ Who helped you to get into this field through networking or otherwise?
- ✓ How important is it to know someone in the industry?
- ✓ What professional associations or organizations are useful to belong to in this field?
- ✓ What magazines, journals, web sites are important to read in this field?

Corporate Culture & Expectations

- ✓ What do you do in a typical day?
- ✓ What kind of a salary can I expect in an entry-level position?
- ✓ What are some other jobs in your field that are similar to your own?
- ✓ What terminology or ideas should I remember when I am applying for a job in this field?

Personal

- ✓ Who had the most significant impact on your choosing this career?
- ✓ What are the things you find personally rewarding in your career?
- ✓ What are the things you find frustrating or disappointing?
- ✓ What extra-curricular activities should I pursue to help me prepare for this career area?
- ✓ What kind of volunteer experience would be beneficial?
- ✓ Why did you get into this field?
- ✓ How do you personally balance home and work?
- ✓ What was the most surprising part of your transition from university to work?
- ✓ What do you see as the biggest challenges new graduates face when they enter your industry?

Here are a few other good questions that you can ask you mentor:

1. *What do you know now that you wished you knew when you started?*

   This question can have several responses, so it is a good one to ask. Most of life and a lot of your career is about experience– things you won't know about until you do them. Think of a mentor as your shortcut to find out about these things so you will be better prepared when they occur down the road.

2. *What one thing can I do on a daily or near-daily basis that will help me become a better... ?*

   Many people have learned great habits that would be useful for someone young in their career to pick-up early. Being exposed to as many of these tips and habits as you can will help you in job interviews and on the job in your career. You never know what valuable habit you might uncover and adopt.

3. *What should I expect to do in this position?*

   As you move up the ladder, you will find out that different positions carry very different responsibilities. You might even find that a position is probably going to be something you may not like. If you know ahead of time, you are able to change course or not accept a job that would have been a bad fit.

4. *What do I need to be able to do to reach the next level?*

   Many positions require a demonstration of certain skills before you can reach certain levels. Asking a mentor what it takes reach various level gives you the knowledge of the skills that you need to demonstrate to show you are ready for your career. You also get a glimpse of a game plan moving forward in your profession.

5. *Do you know anybody in this industry?*

   Think of your mentor as another string in your networking web. You may not know someone who works in a particular industry, but one of your mentors might. If you are interested in working in a specific industry, ask a mentor if they know someone in that industry. You may be able to gain a new mentor to add to your stable, or at the very least, exchange an email or two and get your name in front of important industry pros.

6. *What is the best advice you can give a person interested in this occupation?*

   This is the million-dollar question because it gets right to the point: "What would you do if you were me?" Look for hidden clues in your mentor's answers. They may not really enjoy their own job or profession, and you will want to accurately assess their comments and fit them to your own ideas and understanding. If you like the advice, take it, but it is not required that you agree with everything your mentor has to offer.

How to Repay Your Mentor

Most successful, experienced professionals had mentors once themselves. Most mentors enjoy the intrinsic rewards of mentoring and enjoy helping others. You can foster your mentor's enjoyment by thanking him or her frequently and showing your appreciation for the assistance. Most likely, if you work with your mentor, there will be plenty of opportunities to return a favor or even just take him or her out to lunch.

> *However, one of the best ways you can thank your mentor is to utilize their help, become very successful in your field, and then pay it forward to another former athlete by mentoring their new career some day!*

Chapter 7

Creating A Network That Works

⚾ *Utilizing the Good Ol' Boy Network... Especially if You're a Woman*

Companies determine their hiring needs long before a job opening is formally announced. In many cases, these jobs are never openly advertised. During this time, companies conduct a search to see if anyone within the organization knows of a talented person who might be available. It is during these short windows of opportunity that the networking strategies you learn and deploy will produce some of your greatest opportunities.

Studies consistently show that the most effective job search method and career advancement tool is networking– the art and science of finding job leads through family members, friends, and acquaintances. Over 80% of successful job searches come as a result of knowing someone or something and talking to people. The least effective job search method, which ironically is the most widely used method, is responding to classified ads and job postings on the Internet. Doing the job search as basically a direct-mail operation, many are disappointed to discover the reality– a 2% response rate for direct-mail job hunting is considered successful.

> *In the era of email, Twitter, and text, it may also come as a surprise that the most effective means of communication is still face-to-face and word-of-mouth. And when it comes to finding a job, networking through personally meeting and talking with people is now more important than ever.*

Most athletes that have competed in highly competitive environments operate within a rich network of relationships that have developed over time as they progressed in their athletic career– from coaches, teammates, parents, administrators, alumni, boosters, media, business people, politicians, members of churches and other community organizations. Networking is essential to a successful job search and your key to the hidden opportunities that never get publicized. The community of contacts you assemble throughout your lifetime can provide critical details on job leads, vacancies, and industry trends. They'll also tell you what you'll need to succeed in your search for a new or better job and a rewarding career.

In the final analysis, your network is a group of people who know that you are looking for a job. These people know what skills you possess, what interests you have, and that you are ready to explore new ideas and meet people. When you assemble a career or job network, it usually implies that you are actively looking for a job opening. Networking is not the same as informational interviewing or having a mentor, but you use many of the same techniques in how you manage the relationship.

Networking is increasingly taking on new communication forms in today's high-tech world. Job seekers can take advantage of several websites and electronic databases conducting a job search, gathering information on the job market, and disseminating resumes to employers. The Internet also allows job seekers to network for people, information, advice, and job leads. Several websites will help you develop networking skills, as well as put you in contact with them for employment-related opportunities. These sites include a wealth information on the networking process. As an athlete, you should be certain to register with ***www.careerathletes.com*** and consider opening an account at ***www.linkedin.com***.

The Power of Common Interests and Information

What makes networking work is that everyone is fundamentally comfortable with conversation, sharing of information, and helping another human being. It's 100% natural. When it happens, networking has an easy flow.

When people need information about important matters of daily life, they usually get it by asking around. For instance, when parents need a babysitter, they usually ask other parents. When you need a new doctor or dentist, you might ask around. You probably decide which movies to see or avoid, based on asking around and talking to people, and it is the same with everything from your classes and instructors to which computer or cell phone to buy. Asking around usually provides you with some advance information that enables you to make a more informed decision. We all do this kind of thing all the time, usually without noticing that we are doing it.

All of this is networking… real networking, and not the stuff you read about in some job search article or website. What makes it real is that the two people talking to each other create a kind of shared interest and connection, and an implied trust is developed and shared. The shared interest could be that they are both are athletes or are in the same major. The connection could also be that they have a mutual friend or they share the same university. The key is that they share an interest in someone, something, or somewhere.

Real networking is what happens at parties. You meet someone, and in the first few minutes, you look for a common interest (people, activities, interests, attraction, personality). If there is no common interest to be found, the conversation usually goes nowhere, and you go your separate ways. However, if you find some common interest, the conversation usually takes off.

The other thing that happens in a real network is that people share valuable information. Information is free, but in today's complicated society, it is becoming more common to share the valuable information in one-to-one settings, not over electronic airways. If you are an employer looking for a good addition to your company, it is becoming more valuable to ask current employees for their leads and employee recommendations rather than exclusively relying on job boards or career center advertising.

🏐 Building Your Network

In today's new work economy, successful job seekers and networkers have navigated the break from old-school, passive job search roles (like searching job boards, advertising posts, and random cold calling employers) by orientating themselves towards face-to-face action. Smart athletes now know that it is a first-move requirement in today's job market that they present themselves to their network before anything else– to get a feel of what's going on from many different perspectives and potential introductions that can save valuable time and trouble.

> *Everyone's initial network consists of interacting with individuals whom they are closet to and feel most comfortable around. When you decide it is time to put the word out that you are looking for new or renewed career opportunity, you begin by calling your friends, family, teammates, and coaches. The following are some basic steps that will help you meet people in your field and network with them successfully.*

Building a base of contacts

It's important to remember you are trying to get information from these people, and not necessarily a job. Coming right out and asking friends or associates for a job can put them off and make you sound over-anxious or desperate. Ease into your building your network by:

- ➢ Start talking with friends, your coach, and close teammates. Even if they are not interested or employed in your chosen career, they may have information and contacts that can be useful.

- ➢ Base your approach on how well you know and trust each person. Let him or her know you are looking for a job and you would appreciate advice, ideas, and suggestions. Bring up the subject of your job hunt in general, then ask if you can sit down to discuss it later. This is to enable your friend/acquaintance to prepare in advance.

- ➢ Don't be afraid to call people you have not talked with in a long time; most people are flattered when asked for advice.

- ➢ Be open and go into details about the kind of work and organizations that interest you.

The more people included in your network, the greater the chance that you will hear about job openings. Likewise, the larger your network, the greater the chance that employers will hear about you when they have job openings.

Possible networking contacts

Expanding your basic network will necessitate getting outside your comfort zone and contacting an extended list of individuals and groups. Here are a few ideas where you can certainly identify potential network members if you spend the time and effort!

- ✓ Friends and family
- ✓ Athletic alumni associations
- ✓ Former athletes from teams you've been on
- ✓ In-laws and distant relatives
- ✓ Neighbors (current and past)
- ✓ Social Acquaintances (golf, swim, tennis, social clubs)
- ✓ Classmates (from any level of school)
- ✓ College Alumni (get a list of those living in your job search area)
- ✓ Old roommates, dorm floor pals, sorority or fraternity alumni
- ✓ Clergy and church members
- ✓ Former teachers, professors and administrators
- ✓ Parents of your teammates or children's friends
- ✓ Anyone you wrote a check to in the past year or saw for services: doctor, dentist, pharmacist, optician, lawyer, accountant, insurance agent, travel agent or repair or trades person
- ✓ Real estate agents
- ✓ Financial consultants
- ✓ Stockbrokers
- ✓ People you've worked with as a volunteer
- ✓ Manager of your local bank

Be sure to use the college career development and placement services, even if you only attended that college a short time and did not graduate. Many colleges keep a list of alumni who have agreed to assist current and former students in the job search process. Using this list to identify contacts in a desired target area can save you much time and greatly expand your network

> *Don't be afraid, and don't dismiss anyone from your list just because you have not talked to them for some time. It is common to lose touch with family, friends, and colleagues as life situations change. If the original relationship was valued, your contacts will return your calls, and they will want to help.*

🏈 Prepare to Work at Networking

You will need to create opportunities to talk to all these new people, especially those in different parts of your life other than athletics. The goal of networking is to allow you to communicate your future personal growth plans and interests and to develop face-to-face relationships with many new people that can help you in your career.

We mentioned earlier that one of the advantages to being a student-athlete is that you have an excellent opportunity to expand your network while you are still in competition. Every time you travel to a competition or game, try to meet and make informal contact with some of your opponents and coaches, the family, friends, and relatives of your own teammates, and even referees and umpires. Remarkably, you can expand your network at anytime and almost anywhere– even in places you thought might not be possible.

> *Be sure to find the time to make appointments with your professors so you can learn more about them. You will be amazed at how wonderfully human they are. Getting to know your professors will help you in your classes, as well as when you are in need of letters of recommendation and when you are searching for internships or full-time employment. And don't forget to get to know your advisors, trainers, coaches, and the athletic directors. Each of these individuals has there own individual network and can assist you in much the same way your professors can.*

The primary objective of networking will be that when the time comes, you will inform your network you are conducting a job search campaign. If they haven't heard about your graduations from school, your "retirement" from competitive sports, or your departure from your last job, frame the news in a way that lets them know you are dealing well with the emotions of the situation and you are ready to move on to a new part of your career development. Early in the conversation, reassure the person that the real reason for your contact is to get information and advice– not that you expect them to find you a job. People want to help people, and in the final analysis, people hire people. It's a fact.

Most importantly, get involved. By being active in community, academic, recreational, and social activities, where you can expand your support system and your contact network. You probably have well over fifteen years of competitive athletic experience, so see if you can use some of this athletic experience by seeking out and accepting speaking engagements with local groups who are assisting with a sports event your community. It's a great way to meet parents of young athletes who are potential business owners and hiring managers. In sports, folks tend to look out after their own kind, and you should not underestimate the power of your athletic bonds.

Do's & Don'ts of Networking

> *Here's a simple formula: The more people you network with, plus the more people who know about you and your career interests and capabilities, equals the better chance of thriving in your career. The best business and new career opportunities come through networking. Here are some important steps that can help you make the most of these opportunities:*

1. Communicate clearly

Be ready to describe yourself and your capabilities in a brief, interesting way. Ask a few intelligent, open-ended questions. Share ideas, thoughts, and information. Be both interested and interesting.

Be clear and in the moment and personable but not personal. Keep in mind that cross-gender networking has different body language and conversation styles. Notice the person's tone, posture, hand movements, eye contact, and so forth. For a woman, this is especially tricky landscape so be very aware of the clueless and communicate accordingly.

The first step is to know what you want to do. Before you pick up the phone to begin networking, take a moment to collect your thoughts. Ask yourself, "What do I want?" If it's help, be specific. Do you need ideas, names, or introductions? Make a list of the items that will help you stay focused during your conversation. Most people really want to help you with your job search, but first they must understand what you want. Then they can determine how best to help you.

State your point clearly and succinctly. Always keep in mind that your networking contacts are busy people. Be considerate of their time. Long, rambling dialogs are certain to end your relationship before it ever has a chance to blossom. If you say your call will only take two or three minutes, make certain you stay within that time frame. Anything longer will be perceived as a nuisance call, unless they specifically allow you more time. Your goal should always be to take no longer than three minutes or three leads, whichever comes first.

2. Take notes and exchange information

Bring a notebook and pen or your laptop computer to make a note of the date and time, who you met, where and why, and what you discussed.

If a name or person is mentioned that you think might be helpful to you, always ask permission to use a name. Suppose you visited a contact to conduct an information interview– a short, friendly question-and-answer session designed to help you learn more about a profession or company. Your contact gives you the names of several referrals. Before you leave, ask permission to use your contact's name as the original source. He or she may want to con-tact the referrals first, which will make your calls proceed more smoothly. But the main reason for asking permission is common courtesy. When you mention names, you are capitalizing on your contact's rank and reputation within the business world, so you want to make sure you have his or her knowledge and approval.

Toward the end of your initial meeting, exchange business cards and contact information. By that time, you will usually know if you want to add the person to your networking list. Do not tolerate people whose behavior is questionable. In addition, if you initiated the contact, offer to pick up the tab. It's the right thing to do even if you're broke.

3. Follow-up

Never underestimate the power of a thank-you note. It is very important to acknowledge leads and referrals with notes of thanks by email, phone, or handwritten cards. If a busy executive takes time to meet you and assist with your job quest, acknowledge the help you receive with a handwritten note. This lets him or her know you understand and appreciate their effort and contribution. It also allows you to provide a short progress report and feedback about the referrals. Last but not least, it paves the way for future contact.

Follow-up and follow-through is the key to successful networking. If you have promised to deliver something to someone in your network, be certain to follow through. When you send a card, add a coupon or discount for your business services inside (if possible). If it's a referral to a major contact or if someone was incredible instrumental in helping you get a job, send a gift.

Value your networking contacts and treat them appropriately. Don't drop a potential network member because the timing is off. Next year may be better time to contact them. Make room for new contacts as your network changes and grows.

Regularly refer to your networking contacts to keep your contacts in the networking loop, and stay in touch even if you don't need anything.

4. Build relationships slowly

The essence of effective networking is building relationships– not using people. Networks are based on trust, respect, and personal chemistry; they are not developed overnight. Networking is a give-and-take relationship that is built over time. It is not a job-referral source, even though you will be introduced to potential job opportunities. It is not a sales plan, even though network generally leads to new customers. When someone in your network helps you, you, in turn, help them.

Try to get in the habit of building in more time at the beginning or end of your day to strengthen your networking relationships. Also, select the events or activities that are most apt to bring you helpful contacts. Find out in advance who will be at each one and then decide whether to invest your time and money to be there.

Always remember that you are trying to enhance a personal relationship, learn from your contacts expertise, and be remembered favorably. Listen carefully and do not personally interrogate the person.

5. *Find a coach or mentor*

> *While I think this is a good idea for almost every transitioning athlete, this is essential for women in business, especially home-based or small businesses. To have someone to talk with about your business and career gives you someone with whom to talk and ask questions. Former athletes have usually had a coach at their side throughout their athletic career– someone who can who inspire you to success, as well as provide you advice and information when you need it. Your career is not much different, and many athletes do not do well in sole practitioner, individual environments, unless they can bounce ideas off someone.*

6. *Connect with confidence*

Forget your childhood lessons about not talking to strangers. In business or career development settings, talking to new people is now a requirement to generate interest and support for yourself and your job search and career development. When you are networking in a large, unfamiliar setting like a job fair or networking event, you can skip the formal introductions; this is the time to deal with the challenge directly by walking up to people you don't know, introducing yourself, and starting a purposeful conversation. You can do this if you have prepared in advance, but it does not come easily for most people.

It may not be your style to be pushy, but you will not come across as overly aggressive if you seek out the approachable people. They are usually the ones who are standing alone or who are speaking groups of three or more. Don't be afraid to walk up and say "Hello" or ask, "May I join your discussion?" Don't take it personally if someone doesn't respond favorably to your approach. When you get a cold shoulder, smile, move on and say to yourself, "Next?". Neither men nor women will have their motives misinterpreted in the context of professional networking if they present themselves professionally and if they keep the conversation focused on business issues or topics that are not personal or private.

> *Remember that you're never too old or successful to network. Don't think that executives or others in authority positions are uninterested or unreachable. Many senior executives are delighted to be contacted and want to share the knowledge they've acquired over the years. Because of their seniority, they may be isolated and appreciate the chance to help you. Then, when it's your turn to help someone out, you can react in kind. Helping others in a reciprocal way can be very enjoyable, not to mention the deep sense of satisfaction this brings into your life.*

So, connect with confidence and courtesy on every occasion you think of. The results will be reflected in the growth and strength of your network.

Chapter 8

Winning Resumes and Cover Letters

ⓨ *Your Resume is Your Calling Card*

There are a couple of persistent myths about resumes.

The first myth is that a good resume is a key to getting job. This is simply not true. The resume is merely your calling card; it provides a prospective employer with a snapshot of your background and skills. While resumes play important role in the job search process, they are often overrated. The key to getting a job is a job interview. A good resume is the key to getting the job interview– not getting a job. The bottom line is, if you don't get a job interview, you won't get a job, good resume or not.

Another myth about the resume is that you should emphasize your work history. Again, not true. Employers are interested in hiring your future rather than your past. Therefore, your resume should emphasize the skills and abilities you will bring to the job as well as your interests and goals. Letting prospective employers know what you are likely to do for them in the future will set you apart from your competition.

Competitive athletes who are accustomed to doing rather than telling find it difficult to take an assessment of their skills that transfer to the work environment. But this important step in the job search process, the resume, is the most important step you will take as you begin the transition from sports. While there is no one right way to present your skills in a resume format, there are plenty of wrong ways, and everybody has to go through the step of preparing an effective resume that will help you get your foot in the door with a job interview.

> *Many students and athletes feel they are too young to start working on a resume. On the contrary, even for college freshmen, it's not too early to begin your resume. If you have not prepared a resume, the time is right to get one started and begin to build on it with each passing semester or year. If you make an effort to constantly update and refine your resume, you are guaranteed that it will be a complete and effective document by the time you leave the world of sports and head off into the working world. Your resume has one goal: to get you interviews. It has to make the strongest possible case for your candidacy and create an image that will make people want to meet you.*

Potential employers are looking for people who have clear ideas about themselves and what they do best. You need to prove with evidence that you have provided value in the past that is consistent with the value you will provide your new employer in the future. Initially, this is the job of a good resume.

In Short... Employers Need To Know:

- ✓ What value do you represent to me?
- ✓ What specifically makes up this value?
- ✓ You can do the job.
- ✓ You have a positive work attitude.
- ✓ You are interested in doing the work.
- ✓ You are a good fit within the company's culture and environment.

If successful, your resume will become a powerful marketing tool that promotes who you are, what you want to do, and the value you will bring to an organization. A good resume is the one that is tailormade to a specific job or career field– one that fits your specific background, your unique contributions, your personal and professional goals, and takes a close look at the transferable skills you acquired throughout your competitive athletic experience.

Whether this is fair or not, the fact of the matter is that the fate of your resume is often decided in as little as seven to twelve seconds. Employers receive hundreds of resumes for a single job opening, and 95% of them don't survive the initial cut. Resumes are rejected quickly or screened out to reduce the number down to a manageable level. The smallest mistake– whether missing skills, careless spelling, disorganized content, or formatting errors– may be cause to disqualify you and land your resume in "File 13" without so much as another thought about you.

> *While employers generally don't make a decision to hire on the basis of a resume alone, they often use a poorly prepared or presented resume as a basis to reject an applicant without granting an interview.*

Employers regard your resume and cover letter as your best work and indicative of how you'll perform on the job in terms of work ethic, attitude, and willingness to succeed. The goal for job seekers, then, is to prepare a unique resume that will distinguish you from the competition and make an effective presentation of your value to an organization.

Key Resume Rules

The quickest way to catch the readers' eye and make them want to hear more is to show that you can produce value. Your most relevant skills, achievements, education, and experience illustrate this value.

A well presented, informative resume which demonstrates to employers your potential value and abilities in written communication is the most common and effective means of securing an interview. Your resume is a profile of your skills, job experience, and accomplishments.

It is your opportunity to emphasize your strengths, education, and talents and to tell the employer how you can help the company. What you choose to include in your resume should paint a dynamic picture of yourself.

Employers and personnel managers are very busy and tend to rapidly review resumes. Therefore, your resume must quickly catch the reader's attention and make them remember you. Writing a brief, to-the-point description of your related strengths and experience can do this.

As you begin to write your resume, you will work and rework the content and composition, then decide on a format that highlights your strengths and career goals. You should expect to go through several drafts in this process. You can start by writing out an extensive rough draft of your background, identifying your skills and abilities, experiences, knowledge, and accomplishments. Don't worry about the length of the first draft. You will want to arrange all the information about your background in logical groupings and select the most pertinent information.

In most cases, your final resume will be no more than two pages. An effective resume must provide enough information to compare your qualifications with the needs of the job and be organized so that the employer can easily read the most important information at a glance.

The language used to describe your background will be important. Since space is limited, choosing active, positive language with short, direct, succinct phrases will be important. Using terminology familiar to employers will also indicate an understanding of the field while highlighting your abilities.

You must personalize your resume in order to present your qualifications. This will convey your uniqueness to an employer. Since your goal is to stimulate a prospective employer's interest, you want your resume to reflect your personality, strengths, and skills. As an employer scans your resume, you want him or her to become interested in what you can do for their organization.

Your resume should also be a results-oriented, concise document that summarizes your accomplishments for a particular position. To be effective, it must target a specific job and grab the reader's attention with strong selling points on why your skills and background fit the position you are seeking. Remember... the main task of your resume is to secure an interview, not a job.

Visual Appearance of Your Resume

As the old adage goes, "You will never get a second chance to make a good first impression." The visual appearance of a resume is almost as important as its content. This piece of paper will be your first opportunity to present yourself to a potential employer. The type style and organizational layout will convey an image of your personality and professionalism. You are competing with many others, and the look of your resume is a very important first impression. The combination of great content and great design can secure the interview you desire.

> *The fonts, layout, well-organized content, and even the paper stock all contribute to the way you are perceived by hiring managers and the company or organization you are interviewing with. Think of the resume as the first test you must pass in order to get hired for the job and career you want. Here are a few of the important points to consider when preparing your resume:*

Lastly, when writing your own resume, it will be important to maintain consistency throughout. Content, layout, and information will vary, but the manner in which they are presented depends largely upon an individual's style and personal preference. If you use abbreviations in one section, use them throughout each section. If you capitalize a job title, continue this format throughout the document. Providing consistency throughout a resume creates a neat appearance and enhances overall readability.

The Best Resume Format

A good resume provides a true picture of who you are and what you can contribute. There is no right or wrong format, as long as your resume is concise, readable, and presents your qualifications in the best possible light. Resumes usually have three flavors: functional, chronological, or a combination of the two.

A functional resume is created without employment dates or company names and concentrates on your skills and responsibilities. It can be useful if you have changed careers or when current responsibilities do not relate specifically to the job you want. It provides direct experience most relevant to the job you're seeking and de-emphasizes jobs, employment dates, and titles.

> *For the majority of college students, a functional resume that highlights skills is the ticket to getting the interview. As an athlete, I love the functional resume because in almost every important category, an athlete possesses terrific experience they gleaned from their sports experience. It also allows you to describe accomplishments that make you proud, and this will increase your confidence level when you get the opportunity to review your resume with the hiring manager.*

A chronological resume is used most frequently in the work world. Chronological resumes work best for people who have a strong, continuing work history with progressively more responsible positions. These types of resumes usually present material in reverse chronological order, starting with the most recent job and then working backwards, listing employers, dates, and responsibilities. Chronological resumes are ideal for showing the progress you've made in your jobs and throughout your career.

Combination resumes combine the chronological and functional formats to highlight selected jobs. A combination of the two may be used to highlight your experience or accomplishments gained from multiple jobs or career changes.

Sample Athlete Resume Format

YOURFIRST INITIAL. LASTNAME
Your local/school address • Your permanent/parents home address
(xxx) xxx-xxxx cell/text • yourname@college.edu

EDUCATION

University of California, Los Angeles — Graduation June 2011
Bachelor of Arts Candidate, Major in Communications & Minor in Scandinavian
- Cumulative GPA: 3.77
- Expected to Graduate with Honors
- Basic knowledge of Norwegian language
- Alpha Lambda Delta & Phi Eta Sigma Honor Society (2007-Present)
- Athletic Director's Honor Roll (2007-2010)
- UCLA Athletics: All Academic Team (2008-2009)

Summary of Qualifications/Skills
- Ability to organize time well to complete goals
- Ability and desire to work in a team environment
- Coachable and willingness to learn
- Proficient in Microsoft Office: Word, Excel, PowerPoint; Adobe Photoshop

PROFESSIONAL EXPERIENCE

Bruin Woods Family Resort — Lake Arrowhead, CA
Summer/Fall Student Staffer — June 2009 - Nov 2009
- Entertained UCLA alumni at the Alumni Association family camp through facilitating games, activities, and acting in theatrical shows. Accountable to a six-day work schedule that integrated new families each week
- Worked as a lifeguard/aqua fitness instructor; responsible for maintenance, safety and functioning of pool environment
- Maintained a lively attitude in a fast paced environment; developed a deep sense of teamwork among my fellow 50 student staffers and resident managers
- Improved interpersonal skills though proactively establishing guest relationships with kids as well as adults; improved customer service skills by anticipating and providing attention to the needs of guests at any moment

The GAP — City, CA
Sales Associate/Cashier — June 2007 - Sept 2007
- Responsible for extensive knowledge of store design and marketing, product materials, product function and use
- Developed strategies alongside management to improve GapCard sales
- Collected and dispersed varying tenders from customers requiring quick and accurate mathematical assessments, as well as strong interpersonal customer service communication and selling skills

Local Swim Club — City, CA
Lifeguard/Swim Instructor — May 2005 - Sept 2007
- Certified Red Cross First Aid and CPR; Certified Red Cross WSI (Water Safety Instructor)
- Taught people of all ages a range of basic water skills to enhance swim stroke proficiency and water safety
- Supervised a comfortable, safe, and fun environment for both kids and adult membership

EXTRACURRICULAR INVOLVEMENT

Kappa Alpha Theta Sorority — UCLA
Member of the Beta Xi Chapter — Sept 2007- Present
- Attended weekly meetings discussing philanthropic, social, and professional events
- Assisted Philanthropy Chair with annual philanthropy benefitting CASA (Court Appointed Special Advocates)
- Greek Community involvement progressed ability to make decisions, motivate others, organize people, get along with various personalities, and speak in public

Women's Varsity Collegiate Water Polo — UCLA
3-year Team Member — Sept 2007 - Present
- Two-time NCAA Division-1 National Champion
- Bruin Elite: Acosta's Athlete of the Quarter (Winter 2009)
- Committed 30-40 hours a week towards team practices, study hall, tutoring, mentoring and peer leadership

Keywords and Scanned Resumes

A keyword is usually described as any nouns or short phrases that describe your knowledge, skills, and achievements that are important in the position for which you are applying.

Today's resumes have to be prepared in a fashion that is electronically compatible. Companies now scan most resumes, whether you sent it via regular mail or email. It is then added to a company's database, where the employer can search for candidates via keywords. For this reason, you should include as many appropriate keywords or skill words in your resume as possible.

But don't overdo it! Stringing keywords together in a paragraph at the end of your resume so every word that applies to your career will be found is a losing proposition. Rather, work keywords smoothly into the body of your resume. At most small companies, resumes are still screened first by people, and they won't understand why there is a paragraph of seemingly unrelated words at the bottom of a page.

It is in your best interest to utilize keywords throughout your resume, but they are most important in the very beginning. You can determine keywords by reviewing:

- The Dictionary of Occupational Titles
- The Occupational Outlook Handbook
- Industry/Professional and Technical organizations
- Professional/Technical acronyms (i.e., HTML (HyperText Markup Language)
- Buzzwords specific to a profession or industry
- Job postings or classified advertisements
- Local government job service agencies
- Recruiters job descriptions
- People you know who work in the same field

After you make a list of keywords for your resume, write synonyms for them, and include these into your resume where appropriate. This will broaden your chance for electronic selection.

Additionally, you need to know that a scanner reads a page like you do– from left to right– so you will need to eliminate columns or lines in your resume as much as possible. Scanners also have trouble with serif fonts and any gradation or shading, so it's best to avoid these as well.

A standard typeface such as Courier, Arial, or Times with a point size of ten to fourteen is usually best. Use only capital letters or boldface to emphasize important information, and try not to use italics, underlining, boxes, or graphics.

> *Obviously, when you remove all the formatting, it makes your resume look plain. However, after emailing your resume, you can immediately follow up by mailing a distinctive and "prettier" paper resume to the hiring authority. Please note that before you email your resume, look at your email address! If you've chosen an email address name that's other than professional, maybe it's time to select a new email address which may be more appropriate for your career search. For example, inyourface24-7@email.com might not be appropriate for someone looking to be hired in a reputable company.*

What You Should Never Include in Your Resume:

- ✓ Age
- ✓ False information
- ✓ Marital status
- ✓ Health
- ✓ Number of children and their ages
- ✓ Hobbies or dangerous activities (unless job-related)
- ✓ Photographs
- ✓ Race
- ✓ Religion
- ✓ Detailed description of non-relevant jobs
- ✓ Controversial information (i.e., political affiliation)
- ✓ Social Security number
- ✓ Anything Negative

Overcoming No Previous Experience or a Low GPA

Even if you have no practical work experience, a nicely prepared resume that answers the basic needs of an employer can still be the ticket to getting the interview. In every job interview you have, the interviewer will want to see a copy of your resume. A good resume that represents your hard-earned skills and competence acquired thorough your athletic experience will help you bridge the gap between college and the work world.

Some competitive athletes are frustrated because they feel they don't have enough previous employment to allow them to find a decent job. They've heard so much about the importance of practical experience. Others may fear that they're good, but their GPA may keep them from being considered by the companies they really want to work for. There are solutions to these and related problems.

A high grade point average (GPA) is certainly an asset, but it is not a necessity for finding a good job. It's true that certain corporations require a high GPA, and many management training programs with major retail chains require at least a 3.0 for recent grads and students. But once you have been working at a company for two or three years, you are no longer a recent graduate and will not be treated as such, so you can apply to some of the businesses that previously wouldn't look at you. With three years experience, you will probably not be asked for your college transcript, and your GPA will not follow you around the rest of your life.

Cover Letters Count...Probably More Than You Think

If you're like most conscientious job seekers, you put a lot of time and effort into your resume. But have you given your cover letter its proper due? If you haven't, you are missing a valuable document in the whole job search process.

Studies have shown that 86% of executives polled said cover letters are valuable when evaluating job candidates. It seems that everyone is starting to include cover letters, even when they apply electronically. In fact, the same studies show that a whopping eight out of ten (80%!) managers said it is common to receive electronic resumes accompanied by cover letters.

A cover letter is a short introduction letter that accompanies your resume and serves as a formal introduction of you to potential employers. It will inform the employer of your valuable skills and personal attributes that relate to the job. The cover letter should persuade the employer to read your resume. It is especially important in this day and age that a cover letter be included with every resume you send to an employer.

> *Giving your cover letter the attention it deserves improves your chances of capturing a hiring manager's attention. If you're not sure what makes a cover letter great, try these seven suggestions.*

1. Personalize It.

People like to see their own name in print. Instead of addressing your letter, "To whom it may concern," attempt to get the name of the person who is ultimately responsible for the hiring decision. If you don't know the hiring managers name, call the company and ask.

Never address your letter to "Dear Sir or Madam" because this is the equivalent of the junk mail you receive that's coldly labeled "Resident" or "Occupant." Be sure to include the person's correct title and business address.

2. *Get On The Internet With A Goal In Mind.*

Put your ability to crawl the Internet to good use by researching your target company online. In your letter, try to demonstrate how your knowledge and skills fit the job description and how you might add value for that employer.

3. *Bridge The Resume Gap.*

If your resume is a bit sketchy in terms of employment gaps, your cover letter is the place to put a potential employer's mind at ease. Explain how you filled the time during these gaps and mention professional development courses or volunteer activities you may have participated in. This not only shows that you've kept your skills current, but also indicates that you were not just sitting around playing video games in between jobs.

4. *Keep It Concise.*

You should avoid overwhelming a one-page resume with a two-page letter or repeating the contents of the resume in the letter. A well-written cover letter is priceless, while an overwritten cover letter will wind up in the garbage can. The objective of the cover letter is not to outline your entire work career (that's the job of your resume), but highlighting two or three skills that specifically fit the position is a must. Generally, these letters should not be more than three to four short paragraphs in length.

5. *Thoughtfully Express Yourself.*

Conveying genuine interest in the company and the position is the goal of a well-written cover letter. The use of highly descriptive and persuasive sentences will induce a positive response from your reader. Remember to focus on the employer's needs and avoid overusing the word "I." This is about the employer's needs, not yours.

6. *Make The First Move.*

Don't sit passively by after applying for a job; rather, take a proactive stance in your letter and identify potential next steps such as writing "I'll follow up with you next week to discuss meeting in person."

7. *Make No Mistakes.*

Please don't rely on your spell checker program to catch every error, and don't rely on your roommate either (even if they say they are an English major). Before you submit your materials, read them repeatedly. Once you're satisfied that you have made no spelling errors and it sounds okay, have a trusted and rather intelligent friend or mentor read it over just as an added precaution.

8. Take Advantage Of Technology.

If you want to increase the odds that your cover letter will be read, always choose the option to add your cover letter to your resume when applying through online job boards. When emailing application materials to a hiring manager, paste your cover letter within the body of your message.

9. Be Polite And Professional.

Always... Thank the employer or hiring manager for their time and consideration.

Here's the bottom line: Even job search letters, regardless of how you send your resume, should be accompanied by a cover letter. Sometimes they are even more important than resumes themselves. The bottom line is, even though it seems cover letters take time, give them the same attention as your resume... for they may be the only reason your resume gets the attention it deserves from prospective employers.

What About References? Do I Really Need Them?

Though serious job seekers devote many hours to perfecting their resumes and cover letters, they often get caught flat-footed when a potential employer asks for references. Many simply throw out the names of a few old coaches or bosses and hope for the best, but putting a little more time and effort into the process can provide the extra edge that you will need to make you stand out from the pack.

Good references can make or break a potential hire, and it's always smart to have several to choose from in your arsenal. In general, most hiring managers only ask for three references, but it's smart to have as many as a dozen available so you can offer those that are best able to talk about your strengths for a particular job. After all, if you're applying to a job that is a potential supervisory position, you want a reference who can discuss your leadership capabilities.

If you have them, the best references are always former work managers and supervisors or people who know your capabilities and work ethic. Hiring managers are wise to the fact that if you list teammates, friends, or coworkers as references, they're probably not going be unbiased and completely honest; because most of them won't say anything bad about you, in spite of how true it is.

For this reason, when it comes to references, I suggest you cast the net a little wider than friends, family, and coaches. If you do not make an effort to think of people outside these realms, you may be missing the opportunity to provide potential employers with a true picture of you as a well-rounded individual. I recommend that you ask influential alumni that follow your sport or are former athletes themselves, academic advisors or other members of the athletic department (besides your coach), media directors, compliance officers, or trainers. Professors and department heads (like an intramural director) and people who can speak to all sides of your character, work ethic, skill set, or past job performance are also great references because hiring managers want to know about your potential– not just what you have accomplished.

Once you have chosen your references, you still face the difficult task of asking them without creating an awkward obligation. I recommend email as a good initial tool to avoid this problem. If you ask people directly face-to face, they may be put on the spot and say "yes" even if they don't want to. If you ask by email, they have the option to say "no" gracefully, which is much better than a begrudging "yes" that may lead to a poor reference.

Once the contact has agreed to be your reference, the work's over, right? Not a chance! References need to be cultivated just like anything else. The reference needs to know your skills and interests, the types of companies you will be talking with, and most importantly, the strengths you would like to be played up (though that doesn't mean stretching the truth). I know you know this, but let me say it again: NEVER lie in a work or interview setting! The truth always finds a way out, and usually it is at the completely wrong time, leading straight to the kiss of death and possibly blacklisting in your field regionally or locally.

Be sure to call your references after a job interview and let them know what type of job you are applying for so that they can mention the things you've done that are relevant to that job's requirements. It sounds simple, but if the reference is not aware that certain skills need to be played up, they may forget to mention them all together.

> *One caution about references: As hiring managers become more sophisticated in their networking, you may find more than you bargained for. If you had three prior jobs and you didn't have a good result with one of them, you should know that a well connected hiring manager will get to that one job and ask them about your work anyway.*

Try not to worry a great deal over a bad job experience coming back to haunt you for the rest of your life. Most managers are professional enough to keep their personal feelings out of their recommendations, but some managers may say that they did not like something specific about you. Even these, however, will probably mention what your contribution to the company was and what you did well. However, there's always the possibility that an old employer may give an uncomfortably biased view. You need to be prepared to counteract this with honestly, accuracy, and a good spin on an otherwise bad experience.

The good news is that hiring managers are usually capable of disregarding a single bad review in the light of several favorable ones– yet another reason to make sure all your references are enthusiastic and well prepared.

Try These Extra Tricks

> *Okay, so you're up to date on the latest resume do's and don'ts, you're crafting smart and incisive cover letters to accompany your resume, and you're getting your resume out like crazy. What else can you do? You may be leaving a few essential job search stones unturned. Here are several less well-known ways to get the word out and jump on the job search opportunities. Remember, a job search doesn't leave room for error these days. Details can make all the difference, so it is in your best interest to put every tool to work for you now and put your job search behind you sooner.*

1. Add a signature line to your outgoing email messages.

This reminds your friends and contacts that you are on the job search. Much as they love you, it's easy for our friends to forget our day-to-day priorities, including the job search that feels like a life-or-death situation for you. Add a signature line to your email messages that reminds your friends what you are after.

2. Include your Linkedin (www.linkedin.com) and Career Athletes (www.careerathletes.com) profile URL with your signature.

If you have not gone to Linkedin or Career Athletes and created a professional networking profile, get it together and make that happen. As soon as you set up a free Linkedin profile, you can customize your Linkedin profile URL to something that sounds logical (like www.linkedin.com/yourname). Add this to your new email signature line. Might as well make it easy for people to check out your credentials, as well as for other former employers and coworkers to provide you with publicly viewable recommendations.

3. Make your Facebook page work for you– not against you.

Smart job seekers fill their Facebook pages with useful and relevant information about what they've accomplished and where their strengths are. Using Facebook effectively in a job search requires more than just taking down the party animal photos. Prospective employers are bound to see your online persona, so you may as well make it one that moves the ball forward for you. If you have to keep your party animal photos, develop a separate Facebook account and profile far different from your actual name and job seeking persona.

4. Add a quote to your resume.

Got a favorite quote from a boss or coach who has praised your work? Add it to your resume in place of the tedious "References available on request." Everyone already assumes your references are available. Mention in twenty words or fewer what one of those people actually said about you, and the more specific the kudos, the better.

5. Put a voice on your job search profile.

Too shy to appear on camera? Add an audio file to your Linkedin, Facebook, or other social networking profile to help job search targets and influencers get a feel for who you are, how you think, and how articulate you can be. Buy a headset for a few bucks and download Audacity for free to make high-quality audio files. You can even send your podcasts to iTunes and build a following.

6. Rewrite your resume so it sounds human.

As a career expert, the biggest job search stumbling block I see is a boilerplate, cliché resume that sounds like every other resume. Yank the boilerplate out of your resume and give it a human voice, replacing "results oriented individual" with "I'm happiest solving thorny problems and accomplishing difficult tasks" or whatever human statement describes YOU.

Chapter 9

Job Interviews and What's Important

⚾ *Still the Most Important Hiring Criteria*

Make no mistake about it: the job interview is the most important step in the job search process. Your previous job search activities have assisted you in getting this far, but the interview itself will determine whether you will be invited to additional interviews or offered a position. How you approach the interview will make a difference in the outcome of the interview.

> *Here's a fun fact: research indicates that about 65% of the time, the person hired for a job meets less than 50% of the job qualifications that were initially listed for the job. This means that the best-qualified candidates usually don't get the job! The reason is because job offers are given most frequently to those candidates who, regardless of formal qualifications, sell themselves best during the interview and listen the most.*

Employers still consider an effective interview to be the most important hiring criteria, ranking above GPA, educational level, related work experience, resumes, letters, and recommendations. What you have going for you is the fact that much like the weather, sports in our country is a great common denominator in conversation between all people. Almost every interviewer and hiring manager will ask you about your sports participation and accomplishments, and this serves as an excellent opportunity to communicate all the wonderful soft skills and valuable lessons you have acquired that are transferable to the workplace. Be certain to take advantage of this terrific common denominator and are prepared to expand on the question "How has your competitive sports experience helped prepare you for the workplace?"

While employers used to hire fast and fire slow, more and more employers see the wisdom of doing just the opposite… hiring slow and firing fast. This means there will be more extensive screening of candidates than in the past, focusing on patterns of competence in order to best predict employee behavior. Employers want a perfect fit, and you may have to respond to dozens of questions from multiple people, which will require you to demonstrate your personality, likability, competence, and ability to make thoughtful decisions.

In every stage of your job search, you will want to always communicate a positive image to potential employers. The initial impression you make on your applications, resumes, letters, telephone calls, or informational interviews will determine whether employers are interested in interviewing you face-to-face and offering you a position. Research shows that appearance makes the greatest difference when an evaluator has little information about the other person.

This is precisely the situation you find yourself in at the start of an interview. Appearance is the first thing you communicate to the interviewer(s) before you have a chance to speak, and they will notice how you are dressed and accordingly draw certain conclusions about your personality and competence. If you effectively manage your image, you can convey a marvelous message regarding your authority, credibility, and competence without even opening your mouth.

The Internet is proving to be the perfect medium for facilitating both the job search and hiring processes. Within the very near future, the Internet will play a key role in screening candidates, from doing background checks, administering skills and psychological tests, to conducting interviews via video link. For employers, new Internet-based hiring software will enable them to eliminate many of the costly face-to-face steps currently involved in interviewing candidates. As a result, interviews are becoming more employer-centered, with greater emphasis placed on what you can do for the employer than what they can offer you.

In interviews, it will be just as important for you to consider how your body language speaks as you do the content of your words. Research shows that approximate 65% of all communication is non-verbal, and as humans, we tend to give more credibility to nonverbal than to verbal messages. As a result, regardless of what you say, how you dress, sit, stand, use your hands, or move your head and eyes, will communicate both positive and negative messages. Honesty, intelligence, and likeability– three of the most important values you want to communicate to employers– are primarily communicated non-verbally.

In every interview, there will also be a flurry of questions asked of you. In addition to the standard questions every interviewer asks, more and more employers are asking behavior-based questions to ascertain your ability to make decisions and solve problems relevant to their organization. Additionally, many employers also seek better indicators of your decision-making style, logic, and pattern of performance by conducting situational interviews and/or tests. Here, they might give you hypothetical or real work problems to solve, and they want to see how you actually behave rather than what you say. Preparing in advance for these types of questions will make the process less intimidating and give you a leg-up on other candidates. It's far easier to formulate positive responses to potential questions in the relaxed setting of your living room than it is under the stress and time constraints of the job interview.

Employers Hire People for Their Future, Rather Than Their Past

Employers have expectations of their ideal candidate. Nothing impresses an interviewer more than showing how you can add value to their organization by being alert, exuding confidence and poise, listening and communicating thoughtfully, demonstrating loyalty and commitment to working hard, and portraying a positive personality. With this in mind, you can see how important it is that your job interview shows you meet those expectations and can add great value to their organization. Prove this during your interview, and the job is yours.

> *The cost to hire and train a new employee is a significant expense for an employer, costing anywhere from $5,000 to $30,000. For this reason, employers will attempt to get the best value for their money. A good interviewer will consciously and subconsciously be asking themselves three questions about you:*

1. Do you look like the right person?

- Personal appearance
- Completed paperwork… A well prepared resume
- Interview behavior
- Verbal skills

2. Can you be counted on?

- Good attendance
- Loyal
- Dependable and completing things
- Productive

3. Can you do the job?

- Job-related skills
- Previous experience
- Training
- Education
- Volunteer work
- Life experiences
- Interests
- Hobbies
- Successes

Preparation is the Key

Before a big game or competition, do you prepare mentally as well as physically? A consistent process of mentally preparing for special events is important. You need to be in the right frame of mind before the clock starts ticking or the starting gun explodes. The same is true for a job interview.

> *Preparation is the most important first step to interviewing. A well-prepared presentation supported by facts and examples can create a very favorable impression. The five top tips that you can learn on any job interview are:*

1. Thoroughly research organizations in advance of your interview.

Don't waste time during an interview by spending too much time on issues that could have been answered by reading the company's literature and/or by viewing its videotape. Displaying your knowledge about a potential employer will greatly enhance your chances of interview success.

2. Define your career goals and the opportunities you want.

One of the keys to making a successful sale is product knowledge. In the case of job interviews, that product is you. You need to perform a thorough self-evaluation well in advance of your interviews. Know what your strengths, weaknesses, skills, and abilities are, and be prepared to discuss them in the interview. You will be asked about them.

3. Be enthusiastic and sincere during your interviews.

It is important for you to convey a genuine sense of interest in the interview. You must appear flexible but not too rehearsed. Even seasoned pros can have interview jitters, but don't fixate on how nervous you are. Above all, never be late for an interview appointment.

4. Be honest.

Don't claim interest if you really do not intend to work for the organization. Don't lie on your resume or during the interview. Although you should never draw attention to your weaknesses, don't attempt to hide any shortcomings by being untruthful. Learn how to deal with the perceived career weaknesses before your interview by talking to a campus career services professional and/or reading books on job interviewing techniques.

5. Be realistic.

Carefully evaluate what the employer has to offer you and, more importantly, what you have to offer the employer. Don't accept a position that isn't suited to you just because you need a job. Although most salaries have been on the rise, do not set your starting salary expectations too high. The starting salary may seem inordinately low, but if it is for a position that you really want and can do well, you might land the job and have an early salary review that will get you a raise.

🎾 Interview Etiquette

> *When you go for an interview, you're trying to prove that you're fabulous and 100% right for the job. But you're also trying to prove that you're just a regular person, not a cocky athlete, smart ass or know-it-all. You have to appear normal, and that means dressing right, speaking with the best possible body language, and obeying some basic rules of interviewing etiquette. Here they are:*

Appear Likeable

In the end, employers hire people they like and whom they think will interact well on an interpersonal basis with the rest of the existing employees. Therefore, you should communicate that you are likeable candidate who can get along well with others. You can communicate these messages by engaging in several non-verbal behaviors. The most important ones include:

- Sit in your chair with a slight forward leaning towards the interviewer. It should be so slight as to be almost imperceptible. If not overdone, your body language will communicate your interest in what the interviewer is saying.

- Make eye contact frequently, but don't overdo it. Good eye contact establishes rapport with the interviewer, and you will be perceived as more trustworthy if you look at the interviewer as you ask and answer questions.

- A moderate amount of smiling will also help reinforce your positive image. You should smile enough to convey your positive attitude, but not so much that you will not be taken seriously.

- Try to convey interest and enthusiasm through your vocal inflections. Your tone of voice can say a lot about you and how and interested you are in the interviewer and the organization.

Basic Rules Of Dress

One school of thought says men are lucky because they don't have to think much about what to wear when they dress up. The other says a suit and tie are just no fun. As with fashion in general, women have more flexibility than men about what to wear to interviews. But that means more decisions! Women are expected to appear up on current fashion while also keeping conservative and businesslike without abandoning some of their individuality.

> *Conventional wisdom says to dress conservatively and comfortably. What exactly you wear depends on where you're interviewing, but if you want to play it safe (and smart), here are some guidelines for conservative interview dress:*

Conservative dress for men:

- A nice, well-fitting suit, either dark grey or navy blue
- A long-sleeved, all-cotton shirt
- A 100% silk necktie (no outrageous print)
- Plain, dark lace-up or slip-on dress shoes
- High, dark socks that won't slide down
- No jewelry except for your class, championship, or wedding ring

Conservative dress for women:

- A suit or dress in a natural fabric
- No tight or revealing clothes
- Knee-length or longer skirts
- Long-sleeved shirts
- A scarf, if desired
- Little jewelry
- A nice day planner for notes or a purse (but not both)
- Closed-toe pumps or other modest dress shoes

To be fair, you could get laughed out of some offices in an outfit like those described above. While some jobs call for a dark conservative suit, others may demand a more casual or more creative style of dress, particularly for careers in creative industries like publishing, the arts, or advertising. One strategy is to head out to the office where you will be interviewing and take a sneak peek at what people wear around the office. (And as an added bonus, this little field trip will also allow you to map out your route in advance so you won't be late to your interview!)

Personal Hygiene

Regardless of what you wear, you should follow some hard and fast rules about personal hygiene. I probably don't have to remind you of this, but you should shower and wear deodorant. Don't wear perfume or cologne unless you're willing to risk giving your interviewer an allergic attack. Women should wear only a little makeup. Have clean, well-manicured hands, and skip the wild nail polish until after you get the job.

Handshake

The subject of hands leads us to that most important impression maker– the handshake. You know the drill: firm, but not painful. If you want to make sure your hand isn't sweaty when you shake, carry a handkerchief. To keep your hands from being cold, wash them in warm water just before your interview or put them to your cheek right before you shake. And, if you are one of those guys who puts a half-twist in your handshake, drop it and play it straight. If you are a woman who just cannot get a grip on giving a good firm handshake, work on it. Nobody likes a limp handshake– nobody!

Eye Contact And Body Language

When you shake hands and say "hello" to your interviewer, make eye contact and continue to make eye contact throughout the interview. Try not to cross your arms (it's off-putting) or nod persistently or rapidly (it's dismissive). Don't touch your mouth or neck or bite your lips, for these are all signals of low self-confidence. Don't fidget with your jewelry, your fingers, or anything on the interviewer's desk. It's best to sit back in your seat with your back straight, leaning slightly forward to give the impression that you're relaxed but alert.

Your Entrance

Before you even get into the interviewer's office, you can start making a good impression. Be on time, but not more than five minutes early (you can kill extra time by grabbing a cup of coffee somewhere nearby or reading– or praying!– in your car). In the reception area, respond politely and in a friendly way to the receptionist and ask where she or he would like you to wait. Look over your own materials or just visualize the first five minutes of the interview. Be sure to take some deep breaths and try to slow your pace down so you won't sound like Mickey Mouse when you start to talk. When the interviewer ushers you into their office, wait to take a seat until you're invited to do so.

🏈 *The Application Process*

As they say, you are what you write. Always remember the purpose of resumes and letters and job applications: they are to advertise you for job interviews. Resumes, letters, and job applications do not get jobs. What gets you the job is your interview. However, since employers know nothing about you and your competence, you must effectively communicate your value in writing prior to meeting them in person for the critical job interview.

> *Successful job interviews begin with a complete job application. The following tips should help you complete a job application to the expectations of most employers and improve your chances of getting a job interview:*

> **Dress neatly.**
>
> Assume that you will be observed when you complete the application, especially if you are in a small office or company. Since you may end up being interviewed on the spot, dress as if you were going to a job interview. First impressions are always important, be it on application, over the telephone, or in person.

> **An application is your first screening test in more ways than you may think.**

> Read the instructions carefully and follow them completely. If it says "print," then print. If it says "last name first," then write accordingly. Failure to complete an application according to instructions communicates a terrible message that you simply can't follow instructions or you have something to hide. If you lack sufficient information, don't complete the application, since you will be submitting incomplete application, which is another negative.

> **Answer each and every question.**

> It is important to respond to each question. Leave no blanks that could raise questions in the mind of the reviewer about your willingness to disclose information or whether you have something to hide. If the question does not relate to your situation, type or write "N/A" ("not applicable").

> **Handle sensitive questions with tact.**

> An application is not a place to confess all your sins or reveal red flags. Like a resume, an application becomes your calling card to be invited to the interview. Simply write "Please discuss with me" or "Will discuss at the interview" if you possess a conviction or have been fired from a job.

The Main Event – The Interview

Before the all-important face-to-face interview, you may be asked to participate in two types of pre-interviews: the screening interview and the selection interview. Both of these interviews come in a variety of altered types and styles.

Telephone Interviews

The Internet has created a global reach, making it possible for employers to broadcast their job listings all over the world. Telephone screening interviews serve as a very low cost and efficient way to quickly evaluate a candidate's viability for the open position. The primary purpose of this interview is to draw out more information than what is shown on your resume and cover letter. The employer may want to shorten the list of eligible candidates by calling each individual, and employers can quickly eliminate marginal candidates, as well as update job status of each individual.

Preparation and practice for potential questions are the keys to doing your best during this tricky type of interview. You should be very careful of telephone interviews, whether giving or receiving them.

When you get such a telephone call, you have no time to prepare. You may be dripping wet as you step from the shower, or you may have a splitting headache as you pick up the phone. Telephone interviews always seem to occur at bad times. Whatever your situation, put your best foot forward by always being thoroughly prepared. You may want to keep a list of questions near the telephone just in case you receive such a call.

Always remember that body language is eliminated from this setting so you must take a moment to organize your thoughts, give clear and concise answers to questions… and even smile to make sure your voice reflects enthusiasm and a positive attitude. Focus on the caller by avoiding distractions and minimizing background noises. Some interviewers may not call you to set up a telephone appointment. Because of this, you should have your resume, your list of questions, and a pen and note pad conveniently placed near your telephone, ready for their call. Your goal? To be invited to an in person interview.

In-Person Screening Interview

A screening interview is used to determine if you have the necessary qualifications to continue to the next step. Typically conducted by human resources in larger companies or the hiring manager in smaller firms, these tend to be done very quickly. The goal is to screen out as many job applicants as possible. The #1 question that the interviewer will have during the screening interview is, "Will the candidate fit within our organization?" Your goal? To be invited back for a follow-up interview.

The All-Important Face-to-Face Interview

> *Heads-up! The first five minutes of an interview will frequently lead to a decision as to whether or not you are serious candidate. Social poise and an enthusiastic attitude will go a long way in making a positive first impression.*

If you get an interview, you're one of the lucky ones. Generally, out of every hundred resumes a company receives for a job opening, only five to ten candidates are invited to a preliminary interview. Then, only those candidate with the highest score will qualify for second interviews. This continues throughout subsequent interviews until the list is whittled down to about three final candidates. When you reach this point, you can count on having at least two (or as many as five) more final interviews before a candidate is chosen and a job is offered. Talk about being tough to make the team!

Typically, this is how you'll be scored during interviews:

50 %   **Good chemistry.** Can you fit into the organization?

- Grooming/General appearance: Does the candidate fit our image.
- Social fit: Communicates and listens well, is a good fit with coworkers, customers, and management.
- Shared Values: Personal interests and beliefs are consistent with the company's goals and objectives.
- Present/Future/Leadership potential: Honest, mature, stable, likeable, and relates well to others.
- Attitude: Positive and upbeat with a can-do attitude, follows directions and accepts criticism.

30 %   ***Competence and ability.*** Can you do the job?

- ♦ Technical Fit: Has the skills, talents and ability to do the job
- ♦ Expertise: Has the background and experience to do the job
- ♦ Education: Has the required knowledge to do the job

20 %   ***Willingness and enthusiasm.*** Will you do the job?

- ♦ Ambition: Has the desire to learn, grow and excel
- ♦ Intelligent/Energetic/Motivated/Team Player: comprehends and adapts quickly, achievement oriented

Just Don't Stress Out

Ever been nervous? If so, you might have experienced sweaty palms, a sense of lightheadedness, and rambling speech– and as inadvertent as they may be, none of these things will help you make a great impression at a job interview. The good news is that most interviewers already know you're nervous. Even still, there's no need to advertise the fact with tense muscles and a lack of eye contact.

> *Unfortunately, the stressful nature of a job interview can be enough to make almost anyone nervous. But you don't have to worry about a clammy handshake and stammering chatter if you try a few of these simple tricks to calm your nerves:*

- ✓ **Arrive early– very early.**

    Everyone knows you should be a few minutes early for your job interview. But if you're easily disturbed by stressful situations, you should strive to arrive about thirty minutes early. Sit in your car or a nearby coffee shop and use the time to relax. Then head to the restroom to check your clothes and overall appearance. If you feel confident and secure, you'll be less likely to succumb to your nerves.

- ✓ **Smile!**

    Smiling makes you seem friendly and confident, even if you don't feel it! Studies have found that even forcing a smile will make most people feel a little bit happier. When you portray confidence, the interviewer will treat you with respect, which makes it easier to relax your nerves. So smile confidently when you greet the interviewer.

- ✓ **Take a moment to answer.**

    Before you answer any questions, take just one moment to inhale a deep breath and give the question some quick thought. It may seem like an eternity has passed, but it will only be one or two seconds, and your pause will seem like a natural, thoughtful pause. Moreover, the deep breath will help calm you, and preparing the answer in your mind means you'll be less nervous when you speak.

✓ **Look at the interviewer's face.**

If meeting the interviewer's eyes makes you nervous, then stare at the spot right between his/her eyebrows. Avoid staring at noses and mouths, however, since they are below the eyes. Most of us can tell when someone is looking at those parts of our face.

✓ **Relax your body.**

Is there a lull in the conversation? Use that opportunity to assess your body. Are you rigid and tight? Are your muscles clenched? A tightly clenched body will feel tense and stressed. If your muscles are rigid, relax your muscles as much as possible without slumping in your chair. You'll feel and appear more comfortable and confident.

Frequently Asked Questions (FAQs)

Many interviews consist of a combination of light conversation, storytelling and questions/answers exchanged by you and the interviewer. More and more, employers are conducting a different type of interview than they did five or ten years ago, and interviews are now filled with behavior-based and logic questions designed to elicit clear patterns of your behavior and competence relative to the employer's needs. Behavior-based and logic questions are designed to be very specific and challenge you to provide concrete examples of how you think or your achievements in different types of situations, and they generally consist of some variation of the following:

- "Give me an example of a time when you..."
- "Give me an example of how you..."
- "Tell me about how you..."
- "How many windows are there in New York City?"

In a way, these types of questions provide an excellent opportunity for you to sell your positives with an example or two. If you're properly prepared, certainly you can briefly describe a situation in your life (work, school, sports, etc.), enthusiastically explain what you did, and indicate the outcome. If you question is logic-based, you will be asked to think on your feet and express your best guess.

Your overriding objective on any interview (especially one that asks a lot of behavior-based questions) will be to select examples that promote your skills and have a positive outcome. Even if the interviewer asks you about a time when something negative happened, you're goal will be to try to select an example where you were able to turn the situation around and produce something positive from it. For example, if you were asked to tell about a time you made a bad decision, you would try to identify an occasion where even though it wasn't the best decision, you were able to learn from it or pull something positive out of the situation.

As you prepare for your interview, you will want to consider many of your athletic situations. Focus on those where you:

- Demonstrated leadership
- Solved a problem
- Made a good decision or made a poor decision
- Handled changing circumstances or events
- Met a deadline or missed a deadline
- Worked as part of a team

> *Your long and interesting athletic participation is a gold mine of relevant experiences that are transferable to the workplace. The more you are able to look back and identify the types of skills and experiences you had in athletics and apply them to potential workplace scenarios, the more you will be prove your value to any employer.*

Here are Some Common Interview Questions

The following questions come up in many interviews. As you answer, the interviewer will try to assess your enthusiasm, confidence, and ambition in determining whether you'll fit within their organization's culture and work environment– as well as trying to determine if your answers are honest and genuine.

"Could you tell me a little bit about yourself?"

Although this open-ended question appears fairly straight-forward and easy, it is intimidating to most people. Most don't know what to say or how long they should talk, especially since the interview is just beginning. You should realize that most interviewers use his question not only for information gathering, but also for assessing your poise, style, delivery, and communication ability. Although this question gives you great opportunity to sell yourself, at this stage in the interview, it is better to be concise and low-key. Remember to stick to the key points in answering this and any other question. Try to keep your answers to no more than two minutes in length. If the interviewer needs more information, they'll ask you for it.

"Why did you leave your last employer?" or "Why are you leaving your present job?"

This question does require a long-winded answer, but remember to be positive and not defensive– especially if you left (or are leaving) because of problems with your boss or coworkers. Do not air your frustrations about your previous or current job or the people involved. Perhaps the best answer this question is simply to state that you're seeking greater opportunity, greater challenges, or more responsibility.

"What are your greatest strengths?"

Smile when asked this question. Have a list ready of what you do best. This question is a signal for you describe your strongest attributes and skills, but be sure that you mention the specific assets that are related to the responsibilities of the job you're seeking. Remember the four basic skills to highlight when you talk about your strengths: self-motivation, initiative, ability to work with the team, and willingness to work extra hours to finish the job. Every employer wants to hire these four skills.

"What are your weaknesses?"

This question is potentially more harmful than helpful, and for many people, it is one of the most intimidating. Most interviewers do not expect you to be perfect, nor do they expect you to reveal your true weaknesses. They are just probing for soft spots. How to answer this question takes some practice, but you will want to try to turn this question around and present a personal weakness as a professional strength.

I ask this question often when I interview candidates. Like most interviewers, I really don't appreciate it when candidates give me one of those fake weakness-that–is-really-a-strength answers. For instance, they might answer, "I have a tendency to work too hard" or "Sometimes I am too much of a perfectionist." I usually cut the candidate off mid-sentence and tell them to stop the BS. Of course, I have had candidates also tell me a real weakness that negatively affects their candidacy. For instance, "I am not very detail-oriented" or "I get tired very early and have a hard time focusing after three p.m."

So, how should you answer this question? Well, here is the secret: Give a real weakness that you are already in process of addressing. This does not mean that you have already overcome the weakness. By asking this question, most interviewers want to evaluate whether or not you have the ability to overcome challenges. In most competitive jobs, you will be forced to address your weaknesses. You can`t give up when you are confronted with a difficult situation. In your answer, you might say, "I have very good verbal skills but have always had to work hard in math. This year, I decided to take a math course to help solidify my quantitative foundation." Alternatively, you might say, "I have always been nervous speaking in public. This year, however, I volunteered for a project in which I had to present to the senior management." Both of these answers speak to real weaknesses, yet they also show that you are actively working to address them.

"Why should I hire you?"

Although this blockbuster question presents job candidates with perhaps the best opportunity to sell themselves as an impressive commodity to every prospective employer, few realize what this question covers and how to utilize it effectually. The interviewer who asked this question is really probing for four qualities that will help the employer: your readiness for the job, your ability to handle it, your willingness to work hard at it, and your fitness for the job. The mistake is made when candidates respond to this question by going into great detail of what they hope to gain from the job. This selfcentered response to the question is a big missed opportunity unless you are ready for the question. If you're stuck on some practical examples, it's always a good idea to highlight your good attendance, your ability to get along with others, the fact that you are a quick learner, and that you possess skills for the job. Other positive responses might include that you're friendly, honest, responsible, cooperative, and hard working.

"How do you define success and how will you make our company more successful?"

This is one of those make-or-break questions that oftentimes determines who gets hired. Based on your response, you'll be ratcheted up the interview ladder or eliminated from further consideration.

This is a two-part question. You should begin your answer with your definition of success, such as: "I learned early in my career that it's passion that drives you toward your goals, but it's hard work that produces your success. I constantly strive to improve my performance by questioning today how I could have accomplished more yesterday. This way, I'll always feel my next achievement will be greater than my last."

Now, to the second part of the question, "How will I make your company more successful?" You might answer this question like, "I am confident and can make an immediate contribution in the following ways… " And then state brief examples of your achievement stories that relate directly to the needs of the open position. This enables the interviewer to gauge more accurately how your talents, skills, and accomplishments match up to the qualifications they're looking for.

With a question like this, the interviewer wants to see if the candidate has placed the company's interests before their own. For example, has the candidate adequately researched the company to determine how they can help solve a problem, increase profits, or reduce costs? What value-added benefit will this candidate contribute to the organization? Are the candidate's prior achievements indicative of how successful he or she will be in this position? How valuable can you be to his/her organization?

"What do you consider your most significant accomplishment?"

Your personal characteristics are evident in most everything you do. This question strikes at the very core of who you are. Your response will speak volumes about your own set of personal values. Companies understand this and screen for candidates having favorable interests and attitudes.

The best way to answer this question is to use an achievement story directly related to what you perceive as the major duties and responsibilities of the job for which you are applying. Try to paint a vivid picture of the nature of the problem and how you got involved, the obstacles you overcame, and the final outcome. If you don't have any practical work experience, this is an excellent opportunity to relive a story from your sports that was a significant accomplishment for you as an individual.

This question is not designed to uncover some earth-shattering event, and it may very well be insignificant in the eyes of others, but it presents the interviewer with a glimpse of what you are most proud of. Did accomplishing this deed require taking a risk? Did you have to give up or sacrifice something in order to succeed? What occurred in this one event that filled you with inspiration, drive, and the will to achieve?

"If you think you are such a good salesperson, sell me a new iPod"

In the past, hiring managers enjoyed springing this question on prospective employees– asking them to sell them a suit, a tie, or perhaps even a computer. If you are in sales, you'll need to prepare for this kind of question. What the employer wants to know is how well you think on your feet (or in your seat). Are you creative? Can you take basic sales skills and apply them to everyday objects? Are you easily stumped when customers ask unusual questions? How composed are you in a sales situation?

"Can you think of anything else you would like to add?"

> *It would be a mistake for you to answer "no" to this question unless everything has already been thoroughly covered in the interview... which I doubt. Even if nothing crucial was left out during your interview, it is useful to go over again your strongest areas and establish that you would be the most logical candidate for the opening. This is usually one of the last questions an interviewer has and a signal that you should be ready with your own questions.*

Here are some more typical questions you should be prepared to answer.

- ✓ **"Why do you want to work here?"**

    After you have researched this particular company, you should have one or two main reason why you have interest in the company. Be positive and emphasize how your skills match the job opening.

- ✓ **"Have you ever done this type of work before?"**

    Never answer "no." Mention similar types of tasks and any paid or unpaid experience that closely matches the job opening. Here is another great opportunity to mention your sports participation and education that demonstrates key athlete soft skills and your ability to learn quickly.

- ✓ **"Tell me about your work experience."**

    Relate all paid and unpaid experience to the job opening. Again, emphasize your skills rather than the job you held, especially if you have held very few work positions.

- ✓ **"What would you do if...?"**

    This type of question tests your knowledge of the job. Begin your response with "One of the things I might consider would be..." and then fill in something you might have learned through your company research. This type of response does not commit you to a perfect solution, and the quality of the solution is not nearly as important as the attitude you have. A calm, thoughtful approach to this type of question is best.

✓ **"Have you ever worked under pressure and deadlines?"**

This question usually means pressure and deadlines are part of the job. As an athlete, you have acquired plenty of stressful, time sensitive experiences– sudden-death elimination, bottom of the ninth inning, must win games to get into the playoffs, etc.

✓ **"What are some things that are important to you in the job?"**

Here you want to relate your work values to job opening. All of those terrific values you enjoyed in your sports are transferable to job– like teamwork, performing well, and achieving goals. While important, it's best to leave out money and fame at this part of the interview.

✓ **"What position are you most interested in?"**

If the employer has not provided you a particular job but is interviewing for a number of openings, it is best not give a specific job title in your response. Stick to the skills and interests you possess and give the employer a chance to put you where they think you're the best fit.

✓ **"Do you have any recommendations?"**

Here is where you present copies of letters of recommendation or speak to the types of team honors and awards you might have received. When you present any letters of recommendation, be sure to briefly state who wrote them and hand them to your employer.

✓ **"What makes you think you can do well in this job?"**

Because you know yourself so well, relate your interests, skills, and interest to the job opening. Every employer looks for some confidence in an answer to this question, but don't overdo it. Nobody likes a cocky, over-confident person.

✓ **"What kind of work are you looking for?"**

Be clear and direct in your answer based on the skills, attitudes, and interests you possess. Try not to think of money as the answer to this question and hold out for a great job that matches what you like.

✓ **"What do you hope to be doing in five years?"**

Be prepared for this question. Have some realistic career goals in mind and certainly don't respond by mentioning the amount of money you will be earning or your personal possessions you hope to have acquired.

✓ **"What have you been doing since you left your last job or school?"**

Never say anything other than you took a vacation or took some time off. If you have been unemployed for some time since your last job, be honest. Say, however, that you have been looking for just the right job and mention what you have learned in your job search process.

✓ **"How did you get along with your former boss?"**

Always be positive. If you didn't like the boss or get along well, say something like, "We sometimes had our differences but worked together to get the job done." If you never had a boss, you can substitute the relationship you had with your coach and how that dynamic was built over the time you worked together.

✓ **"How do you feel about working overtime or on weekends?"**

Whether it's completely true or not, "Love it!" comes to mind as the appropriate answer. Never give a negative answer to this tricky question. It always pays to show your willingness to work. If your religious beliefs conflict with the question, be honest and tell the interviewer the background of your beliefs so they get a good idea of the reasons for your answer.

✓ **"What can I do for you?"**

You can answer this question by reiterating what types of skills and interests you possess and showing the employer how you fit into the job opening. After you have done this, you can ask to be included in the

What About Illegal Questions?

Many questions are illegal, but some employers nevertheless still ask them. Some interviewers ask these types of questions just to see how you answer or react under stress. Others may do so out of ignorance of the law. Whatever the case, be prepared to answer these questions with tact. Don't get upset and say "That's an illegal question… I refuse to answer it!"

Consider how you would respond to these questions:

- Are you married, divorced, separated, or single?
- How old are you?
- Do you go to church regularly?
- Do you have many debts?
- Do you own a rent your home/apartment?
- Are you living with anyone?
- Are you a Republican or a Democrat?
- How much do you weigh?

Ask Your Own Questions

Employers are not just looking for qualified candidates to fill their job vacancies. They also want to see drive, enthusiasm, and initiative. Job candidates who are prepared with a list of questions to ask employers will feel more confident and in control of the interview. Another benefit of asking good questions of your interviewer is that the interview becomes more of a two-way process rather than simply passively absorbing information from the employer. Even if you are ultimately unsuccessful in getting a job after an interview, you can learn from your mistakes and endeavor not to repeat them in the future.

> *Interviewers expect candidates to ask intelligent questions concerning the organization and the nature of the work. You may want to write your questions on an index card and take them with you to the interview. While it might be ideal to recall these questions in the flow of the interview, you may need to refer to your list when the interviewer asks if you have any questions. When they do ask, you might do this by saying, "Yes... I jotted down a few questions which I want to make sure I ask you before leaving." Then pull out your card and refer to the questions.*

Having a carefully formulated list of questions during a job interview will impress potential employers and will help set you apart from all the others who may be equally qualified, but not as well prepared with questions. Here are some typical questions that you should consider asking during your interview:

"Could you describe a typical workday?"

This is a very important question and one that will show the employer you are serious about the job by seeking to find out about the daily routine. Have a notebook handy to jot down the hours you would be working and the responsibilities of the position. If the answers are not to your liking, this can help you decide whether this job is right for you. Advertisements may not always meet with your expectations once you attend the job interview, so finding out the answer to this question is important.

"What training or education is needed for this job?"

When you ask about training or education that might be required, you are showing strong indications that you are the sort of potential employee that will be an asset to the company. You are showing that you want to be fully prepared for the job and are willing to undergo further training if necessary to get the job and keep it.

"What are the opportunities for advancement in this job?"

Job candidates who are already asking about career advancement are forward thinkers and not just looking into this as a short-term, temporary position. Longevity is something that is highly prized by employers.

"What personal qualities are required to be successful in this job?"

This question shows the employer that you are interested in fitting in well with the company culture, make a good impression with the company, and contributing to the success of the company's work ethic.

"What advice would you give to someone entering this field?"

People love to give out career advice, especially about jobs that are offered within their company. However, not everyone asks. Asking this type of question shows drive and a willingness to ask for and receive advice that could make a difference in your job performance. It is far better to enter a new job with your eyes wide open rather than having to find your own way, so asking for the employer's advice is one way to achieve a smooth transition into the job.

Additionally, you should consider asking some of these questions if they have not been answered earlier in the interview:

- ✓ Can you tell me about the duties and responsibilities of this job?
- ✓ What's the most important thing I should know about this job and company?
- ✓ How does this position relate to other positions within this organization?
- ✓ How long is this position been in the organization?
- ✓ What would be the ideal type of person for this position? Skills? Personality? Working style? Background?
- ✓ Who would I be working with in this position?
- ✓ What would I be expected to accomplish in the first year?
- ✓ How will I be evaluated?
- ✓ What is the normal salary range for such a position?
- ✓ Based on your experience, what type of problems would someone in this position likely encounter?
- ✓ I'm interested in your career with this organization. When did you start? What are your plans for the future?

🎾 Remember These Do's and Don'ts

In today's tight job market, the four basic skills to highlight in any job interview are:

1. Your self-motivation,
2. Your initiative,

3. Your ability to work with the team, and
4. Your willingness to work extra hours to finish the job.

> *Keep in mind that during an interview, employers want to know about you. The best advice anyone can give you about a job interview is to prepare accordingly. That being said, there are still some Do's and Don'ts that you should follow to help you have the best interview experience:*

Interview Do's

- ✓ Dress appropriate for the job. Do not overdress, but be clean and neat.
- ✓ Tame the hair. If it is a windy day, bring a comb and hit the restroom before the interview.
- ✓ Use mouthwash and/or a mint before you head into the interview. Dry mouth is common when you are nervous and that can present a bad breath episode.
- ✓ Bring another copy of your resume and letters of reference (if you have them) in a file.
- ✓ Be prepared to stay as long as the interview takes. You don't want to appear to be in a rush.
- ✓ Make sure your fingernails are clean. Leave the gardening until the next day.
- ✓ Be well rested. Get plenty of sleep the night before so that you don't look tired.
- ✓ Be friendly to the receptionist--they are the first one to impress.
- ✓ Check yourself for pet hair before leaving for the interview.
- ✓ Know something about the company. Even just a few bits of information will impress an employer.
- ✓ If you believe the employer will know the person who told you about the job, indicate that in the interview.
- ✓ Answer each question completely but don't over elaborate.
- ✓ Smile.
- ✓ Mirror your interviewer. Do not obviously mock, but note your interviewer's body language and follow it subtly. It has been proven that this technique makes one feel comfortable around another.

- ✓ Thank your interviewer before departure and assure them of your sincere interest in the company and job (if you still have interest).

Interview Don'ts

- ✓ No chewing gum, hard candy or mints (dissolve them or get rid of them beforehand).
- ✓ No stilettos, miniskirts or extreme cleavage.
- ✓ Don't sweat (wear a jacket if you're at risk of having sweat rings).
- ✓ Don't bring an overstuffed purse or tote. No brief cases.
- ✓ Leave your cell phone in the car, or at the least, turn it off in the interview.
- ✓ No friends. Go to your interview by yourself.
- ✓ No exposed tattoos or body piercings
- ✓ Earrings: don't wear 4 or 5 sets of pierced earrings. Keep it simple and professional.
- ✓ Don't overdo the make up, hair or jewelry.
- ✓ Don't bring a bottle of water or a cup of coffee with you.
- ✓ Don't wear strong cologne in fact, don't wear any at all. Soap works well.
- ✓ Here's a no-brainer: no alcohol on your breath.
- ✓ Don't show up with chipped fingernail or toenail polish.
- ✓ Don't have coffee or soda right before the interview. It will add to your nerves. If it is offered, decline.
- ✓ Don't smoke right before you go into an interview.
- ✓ Watch your hands -no wringing your hands or fidgeting with items on the desk.
- ✓ Watch your language. You don't want to offend with a curse word or an inappropriate ethnic reference.
- ✓ Don't bring up your list of job requirements.
- ✓ Don't bring up issues on your resume that the interviewer hasn't even brought up such as a gap, or why you left your last job of 8 months.
- ✓ Don't bring up a disgruntlement that you may have over a previous employer or talk about a former coworker in a negative sense.
- ✓ Don't become the interviewer by asking too many questions about the job. What you really want to know before leaving the interview is when they plan to fill the job or when you can expect some communication. If they

haven't provided the salary range in the job listing or they don't ask you for salary requirements, certainly you can ask about the compensation and benefits.

✓ Don't forget to thank your interviewer even if it becomes evident that the job isn't a good fit.

Interview Follow-Up

> *The practice of following up a personal interview cannot be stressed too strongly. Follow-up basically means that within one or two days of your interview, you prepare and send a personal note of thanks to the person or persons who interviewed you. The basic points you want to make in your thank-you note are:*

➤ Your thanks for the opportunity to interview for the position.

➤ Some of the things you feel make you a suitable or qualified candidate.

➤ Your interest in hearing from him or her again.

But what if you interview for a great job, you think it went great, and a couple of weeks go by without hearing anything? You might wonder if it is appropriate to follow-up your follow-up; it is, especially if you were told that you would hear something within that time frame. It's important to remember that employers are fairly busy with other parts of the business and may not be on your schedule. They may have been delayed in making a decision because of travel schedules, customer commitments, or the hire has moved from a top priority to lower importance in the organization (particularly in this day and age of frequent hiring freezes). When something like this happens, simply call (don't email!) and indicate your interest in checking on the timeline for filling the job. Do not allow yourself to sound irritated if you don't hear what you want and don't make the mistake of indicating that you are a serious candidate for another job but that you really like this opportunity better. Playing companies against one another in the battle to get you never goes over well. If the job is meant to be yours, you'll get it– even if it is not on your perfect timeline.

References

If you already have a number of terrific references, make sure you send each one of your references an updated version of your resume and also provide them with a list of your skills, talents, and abilities. Also, make sure you notify them of the companies that may call.

What if you have graduated and never participated in any meaningful work or school activities other than sports? What types of references can you give to prospective employers? Before you go on that first interview, you will need to dig through your past and get a few good references for the job interview.

Your coach or a member of the athletic department administration is a good place to pick up a valuable reference. Typically, these people can talk about your organizational and leadership skills and your ability to work with others and dependability. Professors can also be positive references, but make certain you have a good relationship with them before you ask. A nice reference from your pastor stating you've lead children's choir, headed up mission trips, or started the church's first softball team says a lot more than you think, so don't overlook your community for additional references. And if you've had a summer job or worked during the school year, ask someone you worked closely with to be a reference for you. It does not really matter whether or not the job had anything to do with your field of study.

> *When it comes to references, what most employers are looking for is that you have a few people that will publicly state their support of you. It takes a decent reputation and a good relationship to receive a written reference from someone, not to mention courage on your part to ask for it! Bottom line is employers will probably not contact your references unless they are work-related, but references are still a very important part of the job search process. Cultivate great relationships throughout every part of your life, and getting great job references will be no problem for you.*

Chapter 10

Overcoming Life's Little Screw-ups

🎾 Arrest Records, Poor Credit, Lousy GPA? Ouch!

Smoke a bong, and if you're Michael Phelps, you end up in every newspaper and lose millions of dollars in endorsements. Use performance enhancers supplied by your cousin, and if you're Alex Rodriguez, you're holding news conferences making excuses about having been immature, pressured, or stupid (or any combination of the three). Drink and drive, and if you're Charles Barkley, you're suspended from TNT before spending five days in an Arizona jail. And I don't even want to talk about dogs and Michael Vick or Ben Roethlisberger. The point is, while once protected from the media, athletes in this country are becoming negative news makers all the time, and all athletes– high school, college or elite– should pay close attention to this trend.

Maybe a political protest got out of hand and you were right in the thick of it, replete with overzealous police officers. Maybe a bout with drug or alcohol dependency left you in a crappy financial position with little choice but to start over. Or before you left college, what started as an innocent fraternity prank turned into a shoplifting conviction. Maybe all three occurred, but since you were not a movie star or professional athlete, you didn't have the helpful agent or publicist, a twenty-five points per game NBA scoring average, or a pile of lucrative film offers that would get your career back on track.

> *Let's face it... these days, everybody knows somebody who has made a misstep in life. Some of these little screw-ups may involve drugs, gambling, drinking, fighting, and police or courts. They run the range from just bad luck (wrong place at the wrong time), to the colossally stupid (sexual assault or serious theft). Most involve youthful stupidity. Thankfully, we live in a society that generally forgives those who repent, but that social nicety is fast falling by the wayside.*

In this day and age, there are more police, rules, cameras, security, and television shows like TMZ that will pay a buck for turning in a friend– and more people willing to accept that hard-to-come-by buck. These times call for an increased awareness by athletes that they are in the public spotlight, even when they are not competing.

If life went as our parents would like it to go, we would learn all about life without having to get into trouble. For the most part, that has probably been true in your life– except for that one incident, for those two or three years before you got treatment, or for that one bad business venture where you wound up with too much debt.

Unfortunately, potential employers often seem to live in something of a fantasy world where no one ever gets arrested, no one spends time in jail, no one gets in a financial jam, and no one ever files bankruptcy. Employers these days are concerned with that four-letter word known as R-I-S-K. If you are looking for a new job, how do you convince an employer that the person who was stupid and arrested is not the person they would hire today?

Background Checks

Nowadays, when employers say they are doing a background check, it is not just limited to your Social Security number and your driver's license. They also want to take a look at whether or not you have a questionable past or possibly how much and what type of social information can be found online. Many state and federal government jobs require a background check, and depending on the kind of job, possibly even an extensive investigation for security clearance.

Under federal law, the employer must obtain the applicant's written authorization before any kind of background check is conducted. You can just say "no" if you do not like the idea of background checks; however, that would automatically give the impression that you have something to hide and almost certainly eliminate you from consideration anyway.

> *There are several reasons why employers perform background checks. The types of background checks companies do usually depends on the job, but they typically include the following:*

Employment Verification

Often a potential employer will contact an applicant's past employers. Many states have laws that prohibit employers from intentionally interfering with former employees' attempts to find jobs by giving out false or misleading references, but a former boss can say anything truthful about your performance. However, most companies have a policy to only confirm dates of employment, final salary, and other limited information.

Education Verification

This is done to verify degrees and certifications listed on resumes or applications. Under federal law, specific records such as transcripts and discipline records are confidential and will not be released by schools without the authorization of the student. However, a school may release "directory information," which can include name, address, dates of attendance, and degrees earned.

Drug Screening

Many large corporations have a policy to drug screen all potential employees prior to starting. In this situation, the job offer is contingent on you successfully passing the drug screen.

Credit Checks

This type of check (sometimes called a "consumer report") is most often done by companies where employees have access to money or sensitive or confidential personal and financial information. Some employers also use your credit history to gauge your level of responsibility, believing that if you are not reliable in paying your bills, you will not be a reliable employee.

In addition to your payment history, a credit report typically includes information about your former addresses and previous employers. Employers can use this as one way to verify the accuracy of information you provide on an application or resume.

In cases of serious credit problems, the good news is that Federal law prohibits employers from discriminating against applicants because they have filed for bankruptcy.

Criminal and Motor Vehicle Records

These types of background checks are not as common, but some companies have a policy of checking criminal records. Although arrest information is a matter of public record, in most states employers cannot normally access the arrest record of a potential employee; however, there are some exceptions, such as for law enforcement positions. If the arrest resulted in a conviction, that information can be obtained. In general, civil suits, civil judgments, and records of arrest more than seven years old are not reported. Depending on your state, however, the seven-year limit may not apply to criminal convictions. Companies check motor vehicle records when positions involve the operation of company vehicles and equipment.

Employment Application Accuracy

Some companies verify the accuracy of the information you provided on the employment application, including what you listed as your most recent salary. When you complete the application, make sure all information is accurate.

Social Networks and Online Information

When someone says that you have been "Googled," this means that everything that you have done online over the past few years is available to be seen. For example, have you made any videos lately and placed them online? Do you have any pictures of yourself online that a prospective employer may find a bit questionable? Have you been written up in a newspaper article? It's all there for any nosey employer to look at and draw their own conclusions.

According to studies, more and more employers are using search engines to find out about an individual. Recently, The Society for Human Resource Management conducted a survey and found 43% of its members said they use social networking sites to recruit potential candidates, while 19% said they plan to. More to the point, 47% of these very same members said they used social networking sites to screen applicants and did so before contacting the applicant for the first time.

> *If you have been on a lot of job interviews lately and just can't seem to land one, it could be due to what you have posted on your Facebook or MySpace page. What you do online could actually work to your benefit if what you have showcased highlights some of your abilities and awards. The bottom line is that information about you online will have either a good affect on getting you past the initial job interview or will hold you back, so you should really take the time to think twice about what you are posting and how it will affect your job search and career.*

What Can You Do to Prepare?

You can take the following steps to reduce the chances that you and/or the potential employer will be "surprised" by information found during your background check:

> *Order a copy of your credit report.*

If there is something you do not recognize or that you disagree with, dispute the information with the creditor and/or credit bureau before you have to explain it to the interviewer.

> *Check court records.*

If you have an arrest record or have been involved in court cases, go to the county where this took place and inspect the files. Make sure the information is correct and up to date.

> *Check DMV records.*

Request a copy of your driving record from the Department of Motor Vehicles, especially if you are applying for a job that involves driving.

> *Do your own background check.*

If you want to see what an employer's background check might uncover, hire a company that specializes in such reports to conduct one for you. That way, you can discover if the databases of information vendors contain inaccurate information. Consult the Yellow Pages under "Investigators" or use one of the many online search services to find a service.

> *Ask if your former employer has a policy about the release of personnel and/or employment information.*

Most companies limit the amount of information they will disclose.

The bottom line? Be honest about your background. Many employers will hire good candidates that fit their needs, even if their backgrounds are less than perfect– as long as they didn't lie about it.

🍎 Bad Credit = Bad Apple

More and more companies see credit checks as a valid way to gauge whether a job applicant is up to snuff, partly because of greater security concerns and partly because such reports are easily and quickly accessible thanks to the Internet.

Today, roughly over 35% of companies use credit checks in pre-employment screening. Meanwhile, about 60% of retailers say they use credit checks in pre-employment screening.

The five industries most interested in credit checks are defense, chemical, retail, pharmaceutical, and financial services, according to Experian, one of three credit reporting agencies that sells reports to employers.

> *While there is a large body of evidence that credit scores have nothing to do with job performance, employers say credit checks are a useful part of an overall pre-employment screen. For jobs where there is access to money, it's really a way to help minimize organizational risk. As flawed as it seems, the logic is that if people have a lot of debt or they haven't been paying their bills on time, there's a higher risk that they might be more susceptible to stealing or theft. Of course, it doesn't mean that's always the case, but it's a way to manage risk. Also, companies perceive paying your bills is general indication of honesty.*

Is there something personal in your financial past that you'd rather not explain to a stranger? Bad credit, a bankruptcy, or a proclivity for spending thousands of dollars on your credit card each month? If so, applying for a new job or going after a promotion could put you in a tricky spot, because an employer can easily find out about all of these things.

Before a potential employer can pull your credit history, you must sign a release. The report the company gets will be just like a regular credit report, but some credit services (such as Experian) remove information employers aren't allowed to consider (such as age and marital status). What is going to show up? Delinquencies, bankruptcies, judgments, liens and a list of your loans, mortgages and credit-card accounts– it's all there to be legally seen by prospective employers.

In order to be fully prepared, you'll need to find out what's in your credit report before you start your job search. Obtain a copy of your credit report from each of the three credit services (Equifax, Experian, and TransUnion) so you're not blind sided by an inaccurate item that you don't know about until an interviewer asks. Under an Amendment to the Fair Credit Reporting Act, you can access your credit report for free once every twelve months.

If there's a mistake on your report, contact the creditor that made the error, clear it up, and ask that agency to report the mistake to the three agencies. If there is adverse information about unpaid student loans, charge card bills, or bankruptcies on your report, don't waste your time and money on credit repair schemes. You can't erase the truth from your credit file, but time heals all wounds; most bad credit incidents will disappear from your record after seven years.

What can you say when you're asked about poor credit? Your best bet is to keep your answer short, sweet, and sincere. Acknowledge the error of your ways and assure the hiring manager that there was a one-time problem and you've changed. For instance, you might say, "When I went away to college, I'd never had any experience with credit. I got overextended, and that was wrong, but I learned a lesson and worked hard to pay off all my debts. Since then, I've had clean credit, and I hope this won't hold me back, because I really want to work for your company." Short, sincere, and sweet.

Drinking and Driving (DUI)

DUI is understandably a big deal, and add my name to the long list of people who have told you not to drink and drive.

> *When we think DUI, we think court dates, huge financial expense, supervision, and lost driving privileges, but the employment hurdle might be the biggest deterrent of all to driving under the influence (if anyone stopped to think about that before downing one for the road).*

To most people (and by extension, most hiring managers), a DUI conviction says something about a person's judgment. It can be an especially significant barrier to entry into some of the very sectors which are projected to experience robust job growth over the next few years (such as healthcare and education) and cost you dearly in terms of lost opportunity.

The experts don't have much to say about a DUI other than you should get a criminal lawyer and see what can be done, if anything, to work that thing off your record; because it's deadly for a young person searching for a job to have a felony DUI.

Misdemeanors

You know it and I know it… college is a time when a lot of people make a lot of stupid mistakes. Unfortunately for some, those stupid mistakes don't stop once they have graduated and may continue on for a few years.

Misdemeanors, by definition, are lesser criminal acts and punished as such. They usually are accompanied with a monetary slap on the wrist, some classroom time, perhaps an Alcoholics Anonymous meeting, although repeat offenses may have you spending the night in lockup. It really depends on the class of misdemeanor that you have committed and the state in which you committed the crime. Some states can jail you for up to a year, whereas other states will give you probation.

Petty theft, prostitution, MIP (Minor in Possession), public intoxication, disorderly conduct, trespassing, vandalism, drug possession, and DUI are all types of common misdemeanors. Having lived in a college town, I think it is pretty obvious which of these are more common for the younger crowd.

A big risk today revolves around drug use and drug possession. Even the most seemingly trivial drug offense can stick with you for years– sometimes permanently. In light of today's litigious climate, employers have to be very careful about the people they hire. That's why criminal background checks are fairly common today; there's a huge liability risk for the company if an employee gets into trouble and it's later determined that there was some type of black mark on that person's record about which the employer should have been aware.

Being charged with a misdemeanor does not make you a bad person, but it may impact your job search. Whereas felonies really hurt an applicant, misdemeanors are not nearly as bad. Any company that does a background check will see what you have been convicted of and all the associated details.

The key to overcoming a misdemeanor conviction in the job search process is simple: the hiring manager will expect a straightforward and honest answer. If you've had a DUI, here's the variety of straightforward and honest answer they will expect to hear:

> *"I have a misdemeanor on my record for drunk driving. I was young and just graduating college. I just found out I landed the job I really wanted and went out to celebrate with some friends. Unfortunately, I overdid it and thought I was fit to drive. Luckily, an officer pulled me over. I learned a lot from that lesson and have since cut back on my drinking substantially and haven't driven drunk since."*

By trying to beat around the bush and pretend that you are 100% perfect, you will do yourself more harm than good. Honesty is always the best answer, even if it may not seem like it at the time. It also has a lot to do with the nature of the offense. If you were twenty-two years old and drunk in public, that is a little more understandable and usually won't be an immediate disqualifier for your next job. However, if you did something involving moral depravity such as theft, you have a much harder discussion ahead of you. But, you still have a shot and need to keep going forward.

A large portion of the answer depends on the job you are applying for and the misdemeanor you received. You can be barred from certain jobs by state licensing boards if there's a drug or theft offense on your record. If you are applying for a job as a bank teller, for example, and have a misdemeanor of petty theft as mentioned above, you may have a hard time getting the job. But if you take that same petty theft charge and apply for a job as a computer programmer, you may not face as many obstacles. If you have some sort of domestic violence charge, getting a job as a police officer may be more difficult. This depends on locality, but generally speaking, you are not offered discrimination protections as a misdemeanant or felon.

As I have mentioned, you may incur obstacles in your job search, but you still should be able to find a job somewhere. Just look for a job that does not relate to your misdemeanor and keep your head up. If you need something to keep you afloat, try and do odd jobs for people and companies and build yourself a huge stable of great references to use on your next job interview!

Overcoming a Serious Criminal Conviction

Seeking employment can be very frustrating for a convicted criminal. The application process is almost a cruel joke. Here's how it usually goes:

"Have you ever been convicted of a crime or felony?" is the question. The application goes on to read, "Answering 'yes' to this question does not automatically ban you from the position that you are applying for." Like I said, it's a cruel joke. The reality is that although answering "yes" to this question is required if you have been convicted, the end result of answering "yes" is always a trash-ticket for that application. It never ends with you getting a callback for an interview. Usually in cases like this, you will receive a letter that says something to the effect of "Due to information on your background report, we are unable to offer you a position at this time." What is the point in conducting a background check if you already explained your situation on the application?

> *Many choices you make in life will determine your destiny for the rest of your life. I personally believe that mistakes are supposed to shape us into more productive people. However, second chances are becoming rare these days, and this bodes the question: if never given a second chance, how can you show that you have learned from your bad choices or your youthful stupidity without constantly being reminded of it and penalized by it?*

Here's the reality: convicted persons are not in a protected class. According to Title VII of the Civil Rights Act of 1964, employers are prohibited from discriminating in employment decisions on the basis of race, color, gender, national origin, or religion… but not convictions. To its credit, the Equal Employment Opportunity Commission (EEOC) has determined that personnel policies that exclude individuals from employment on the basis of their arrest and conviction records may violate Title VII, because such policies disproportionately exclude minorities, in light of statistics showing they are arrested and convicted at a rate significantly in excess of their representation in the population. The EEOC has also noted in its policy directive regarding the consideration of conviction records in the hiring process that four relevant factors should be used when an employer assesses the job-relatedness of an applicant's conviction record:

1. The nature, number, and circumstances of the offenses for which the individual was convicted;
2. The length of time intervening between the conviction for the offense(s) and the employment decision;
3. The individual's overall employment history; and,
4. The individual's efforts at rehabilitation.

However, the bad news is that most employers ignore these policies.

If you've been convicted of a crime, and perhaps served jail time, it might be more difficult for you to get a job. Employers are wary about hiring convicted criminals, and they will often pass on a candidate for only that reason, regardless of his or her skills and education. So how do you get a job after a criminal conviction? There is no sure way, but as an athlete, you have a better chance than most non-athletes, as you are a member of a very close fraternity of former athletes.

Here are some of the best ways you can begin to leave the past behind:

Learn a New Trade

Pursuing an education after a criminal conviction is a great way to increase your chances of getting a job. Employers want to see that you are motivated and determined, and when you take classes or complete a degree, you show you aren't going to allow your criminal past to stop you from succeeding in this world. This will also give you an opportunity to spin your life in a different direction, whether you want to become a bike mechanic or an aircraft inspector.

Set Realistic Goals

It is important for you to realize that your criminal conviction is going to keep you from obtaining certain forms of employment. For example, if you were convicted of theft, most retail outlets are going to tell you "no." This is because you present a risk and liability the employer isn't willing to assume. For many people, labor-intensive jobs are the best way to go because the employers are less discerning. Construction jobs are particularly popular while former law violators get their footing.

Dress The Part

First impressions are extremely important, even when your resume is undermined with the label "convict." Make sure you wear a nice suit to interviews with no exposed tattoos or piercings. Dresses and skirt suits help women to appear less threatening after a criminal conviction. If you want to get a job, you'll have to dress the part of the employee you want to be, so swallow your pride and go buy a suit. Also, studies show that navy is an honest color.

Put It On The Table

No one wants to talk about their indiscretions of the past, but your employer has to know about your criminal conviction. You can either tell them up front, or they can find out during the course of a background check; the latter method is far less appealing. Make sure they know that you've been convicted of a crime, the nature of the crime, and your punishment during the interview. Remember to explain what you have learned from the experience and how you've changed.

Express Your Goals

Employers are always looking for candidates who want to remain in a company long term. To help you get a job after a criminal conviction, make it clear that you're looking for long-term employment. Explain that you want a stable lifestyle now that you've paid your debt to society. And don't be afraid to let the interviewer know that you're willing to work twice as hard to prove yourself. In this way, your conviction may actually work for you, for once.

Come Clean If You Have To

Not everyone possesses the skill of being sincere. But sometimes it's important to demonstrate what you've learned from your past mistakes. I think I speak for a lot of Americans who are fed up with phony baloney, insincere, prepared apologies for something they did wrong. If you've made a mistake, take responsibility for it. What made you make a bad decision? Admit that you knew the risks and, more importantly, the benefits. You might also admit that you thought you were invincible or that you wouldn't get caught. Honesty, while painful, says a lot about a person. You may not get the job, but at the very least, you will feel better about yourself.

Overcoming Your Screw-Up

So what's a job seeker with bad credit, a conviction for a youthful indiscretion, or a six-month employment gap to do? My advice is always to tell the truth no matter what the stakes. Being caught in an untruth is worse than being honest, and oftentimes you can explain your situation in advance.

> *Your interviewer is human, and chances are they know that poor credit can sneak up on you, that teenagers do stupid things, and that people are sometimes out of work. Be ready with a contrite explanation that admits your fault in whatever screw-up has occurred, be prepared to show how you rectified the problem, and then bring the conversation back to why you're right for the current position.*

If that strategy doesn't work, seek work with a firm that doesn't do background checks– like small firms and temporary agencies.

Here are six pieces of my best advice for getting through some of life's little screw-ups:

1. Forewarned is forearmed.

What that means is if you've been in trouble with the law or have credit issues or other negative events that might become known to an employer, research them yourself in detail and find out everything you need to know to fight back.

If you have criminal issues in your past, find out the laws in your state governing what a potential employer can and cannot ask you concerning criminal records. For instance, in California, potential employers cannot ask you about arrests that did not lead to conviction; nor can they ask about misdemeanors. So unless you have a felony conviction, a California employer shouldn't be asking too much. But be sure you know about exceptions to the law. For example, in California, if you are applying for a job considered to be a "secure" job (i.e., a security guard, some banking jobs, and some utility jobs), a potential employer can ask about otherwise excluded information. Check with your state Department of Labor and/ or Department of Corrections about the laws in your state or consult with an attorney.

Also, check the laws in your state regarding your rights as they relate to disclosure of minor drug offenses. Depending on where you live, employers may not be able to ask about specific minor drug offenses that took place more than a few years ago.

If you've screwed up at school, find out what the school policy is regarding disclosure of student records and disciplinary measures or penalties that were imposed upon you. There is no sense coming clean on items or incidents not made available in official documents, so be certain you become very aware of what has been recorded and what is the current policy for disclosure.

2. When you fill out your job application, don't write down any more than you are required to on the application.

Keep any mention of a criminal record or bankruptcy limited to only when asked, and even then, only provide the most basic information. Ideally, check that ominous little "Yes" box and, when pressed for more details (e.g. conviction, year, etc.) write, "More information available at interview." You want to be honest, but you don't want to screen yourself out of the job before you have had a chance to show that any mistakes you made are long past.

3. Think about what industries or professions might be more willing to forgive your past indiscretions.

If you were convicted on drug charges, hospitals might not be all that keen on hiring you, but an office job with routine drug screening might be more forgiving. If it was the political protest that got you in trouble, a nonprofit employer might understand (or even appreciate) your activism, while a bank would shudder at the thought of your participation in any demonstration at all. Focus on potential employers who would take the least amount of risk in giving you a chance.

4. Think about what you learned from your mistake(s) and how your employer would benefit.

What lessons did you learn? What skills have you picked up in the process? Rehearse what you might say in an interview if you are asked about it: "Yes, Ms. Interviewer, I was convicted of assault. In the heat of a protest, I punched someone. I felt ashamed after I did it and realized I needed to improve my communication skills and my reaction to confrontation. After that episode, I took courses in debate, verbal confrontation, and non-violent problem-solving. I now also speak to high school kids about how not to let disagreements escalate into violence. And as an employee, I excel in getting my colleagues to come to a consensus without rancor or office politics." Note the answer has two key elements: a) Taking responsibility for what you did; and b) Explaining the efforts you have made to learn from it. Here's the trick: if you don't take responsibility, most people (potential employers included) will assume you are going to make the same mistake again. If you don't explain the efforts you have made to learn from it, then any apology sounds weak and half-hearted.

5. Be sure you know whether an incident can be expunged from your record.

Bankruptcies usually remain on your credit record for seven to ten years.

Criminal records may or may not be expunged, depending on the state you live in and the Statute of Limitations. Don't assume that because you were under eighteen when the crime was committed, it will never show up to haunt you. Again, check with your state Department of Corrections or Department of Labor.

6. Search engine capabilities continue to grow at record rates.

If you are wondering how your prospective employer knew all about you when you went for your job interview, there is a huge possibility that you have been Googled. To put this into better perspective, our friends at Google only search roughly 15% of all the available data that is on the Internet– only 15%! In Silicon Valley, there are new startups every month that have received venture capital to develop new search capabilities with specialized focuses. The future will soon reveal almost everything to potential employers, so remember that your actions today will be very important tomorrow.

> *The bottom line is, if you're pursuing an opportunity, don't lie about your record. Depending on the industry, if an employer knows you did something stupid when you were younger and have had a clean record ever since, they may very well overlook it and offer you the job anyway. If you lie on your application (a legal document) and the company finds out you were dishonest when they run the background check, you're guaranteed not to get the job; and if they hired you, they will fire you.*

Chapter 11

Tips from the Pros

🏐 *Career Pointers From Former Collegiate Athletes*

The transition from a lifetime of competitive sports to a successful work and career environment is a tricky road filled with opportunity and pitfalls. Every collegiate athlete has to go through it, and so will you.

Recently, over 300 former collegiate, elite and professional male and female athletes were polled and asked to answer (in their own words) three basic questions about their experiences as an athlete and the effects it had in their career development. Generally, these athletes have all been very successful in making the transition from competitive sports. It's also very interesting that when I asked them to dissect their success, they uniformly attribute their athletic experiences as the key differentiator in their job search, interviews and, ultimately, their career success. Many of these athletes also cite similar beliefs as to what is important in life and in a successful career. Hopefully, this representative sample of advice and wisdom from these athletes will be something from which you can significantly benefit.

1. What advice would you give a current college athlete?

Knowing what you know today, what advice would you give a college athlete who is tracking towards completing their eligibility and is looking to make their mark (and find fulfillment) in a profession?

2. What real world advice do you have on finding a career?

What's really important (real world advice... .good or bad) in finding, creating and flourishing in a career?

3. What specific skills did you acquire as a competitive athlete that helps you in your career?

Can you list specific skills that were learned from competitive athletics that directly enhance (and how they enhance) your career, even today? What additional message(s) would you like to express to men and women competitive athletes today as it applies to 'life after sports' (traps, tricks, wisdom, discipline, expectations, etc.)?

When you read over these comments, you might be able to gain some valuable insight into your own particular thoughts on career development and life after sports. You might read a comment that pertains to your current situation right now, or perhaps another comment might allow you to put your own experiences and thoughts into better perspective.

There is a check box before each career pointer for you to rate how important each is to your own career situation. Mark each career pointer with either 1-2-3-4-5, with 1 being most valuable to you. You can always return to this list, but pay close attention to the 1s and 2s, and integrate this wisdom into your own job search, interviews, or career development plan.

What Advice Would You Give A Current College Athlete?

"Knowing what you know today, what advice would you give a college athlete who is tracking towards completing their eligibility and is looking to make their mark (and find fulfillment) in a profession?"

- ☐ Stay the course when you find it. Everything in life takes effort for resounding benefits to come.

- ☐ I would remind them that this time in sports is the best time of their lives, but that they will need to put an equal effort into their job search. In picking their job, they must realize that their job should have some component of doing what they love.

- ☐ Try to get as many different internships as possible during college. You won't be able to really know what you like or dislike if you don't have some experience. And don't worry about the money… it's better to do the work for free when you're young, rather than be stuck in a paying job later that you hate.

- ☐ When it comes to classes, take as many different types as possible. And find a little time to read before you hit the interview trail, preferably business non-fiction and newspapers. Become an interested, global citizen, and know what's going on in the world today.

- ☐ Be who you are and don't try to be someone you're not. You can learn from others but you have to incorporate that into your own personality. Be honest and up front with yourself and others about your goals. Your reputation is most important so be consistent.

- ☐ Your education and finishing your degree is important not only to yourself, but to your family and those who in the future may employ you. Social skills learned during your higher education years will serve you through your beginning career to your latter years. Friends and family are the gold in your life. You never know when or where you will cross paths with someone you competed with or against, and when you need it most, those friendships will have the most meaning and importance.

- ☐ Learn to use the phone rather than email or text if you can. Call everyone back the same day you get his or her message. Nothing… and I mean nothing is better than a talking directly to someone who is important, you respect or you love.

- Athletics was such a huge part of my schooling that I didn't always feel that my actual education was going to land me the job of my dreams. I didn't even know what I wanted to do! With my personality and work ethic, I did know however that I could do anything I wanted and I would put 100% effort into things I enjoyed. As you leave college and start discovering what is out there, the people you know and the relationships you make during college will help you get take those first steps into the working world. Don't expect to find your favorite job right out of the chutes. Use your friends, family, and their family to make connections to possible jobs that are out there that may be of some interest to you.

- The advice I would give is to look at doing a variety of internships. That's what helped me find jobs and know what I wanted to do. Through internships, I learned whether or not a sales type of job or a analyst job was for me. I learned quickly that there was no way I was going to spend my life in a cubicle crunching numbers, that the best route for me was to be out meeting and talking with people. So in trying different types of internships you can start to rule out what kind of person you are and what kind of job type works for you. The second piece of advice is to find a few people you admire and see as successful and sit and have discussions with them about their career paths and any advice that they may have for you. Why not learn from other people's mistakes?

- Don't take forever getting the degree finished. Don't fall for the siren's song of "gee, I just spent four years busting my ass so now I'll go surfing for a few years". The key edge you earned by being a competitive college athlete is one of your best selling tools. Once you stop competing, you will start to lose that edge. There will be no fulfillment without sacrifice and hard times. Fulfillment in business has the same source as fulfillment in competition: The harder you work, the more you win.

- Competing in collegiate athletics and still getting a degree is the ultimate multi-task. Apply the same daily dedication that became innate as an athlete towards your career. The athletic rush is hard to replicate but it also provides you with an uncommon inner drive that people envy and want to be around.

- People generally don't care how many points you scored in a game, they want to know what type of people skills you have, what your work ethic is like, and how responsible are you.

- Try to learn what you can about potential professions before you're out of school. Get an internship, volunteer, etc, even if it's just a few hours a week his can help you learn about different professions and make many contacts. Also, don't be too worried about getting into to a profession that you feel you're "supposed" to gravitate towards because of your degree, etc. If you know you like a certain area of work, it's worth paying some dues for a few years.

- Living off sports is short-lived. Leveraging sports is a tool for life.

- I believe that it is very important to find balance in your life including the balance between academic, athletic, professional and personal endeavors. I remember when I was finishing my athletic eligibility, I was looking forward at my life where swimming was still an important part of what I do, but did not define me. Similarly, I did not want work or any single aspect of my life to define the entirety of me I found a good balance as I transitioned to graduate school and then to my career.

- [ ] Work hard to get the best grades that you can. Academic achievement will stand out on your resume, and it will also open the door to graduate school if that's a path you want or need (e.g., for careers in medicine, law, etc.) to take.

- [ ] What kind of people do you want to work with and, more importantly, work for? Find an organization with those kinds of people or a boss who you like and respect and you will likely have found a situation analogous to playing on a team with great coaching. The same two factors should be front and center when thinking about a profession. What kinds of day-to-day activities do you enjoy doing? Interacting with people, analyzing information, having an immediate scorecard about how you are doing, working with your hands, being able to see results immediately, etc. That is analogous to finding the sport that you love.

- [ ] Don't worry about what your ultimate profession will be. The most interesting people have no idea where they will be in 10 years, and neither should you.

- [ ] Emphasize your athletic accomplishments! Do not minimize something to which you've devoted so much time, energy and passion. Most people will appreciate your efforts. However, when it gets to the personal interview level, "Read the Room"...... not all people care, in fact, some resent athletes.

- [ ] If you're lucky enough to know what it is you want to do for the rest of your life, pursue that industry, get a foot in the door, any foot in any door, gain experience, and develop an employment history.

- [ ] Try many different things. For too long I took classes others suggested that fit my schedule, that looked easy, etc. Once I went to graduate school I began taking classes that looked interesting, aroused my curiosity, and that were about unknowns I wished to explore.

- [ ] Feed your curiosity. Now that I teach high school students, one thing I mourn is that I see too many who don't listen to and feed their curiosity, who don't know how to listen to their own minds, and who are so easily swept up by shallowness. I think we have to practice being curious and feeding our minds. Find the curiosity and then the profession that allows you to make a living, not the other way around.

- [ ] It is so hard to know what profession you will truly excel at, until you go out and try, fail and succeed. Very few are fortunate enough to have the foresight, vision, and tools to make their dream job happen right after they graduate. So make sure you do not piss any one off along the way that you might in turn have to ask advice or for a favor.

- [ ] The business world works just like a sports team. There are team owners, coaches, stars and support players in every business. Like sports, in business everyone gets to choose how hard they want to work, whether they want to be a team player or an individual player, what they will do to succeed and how far they want to go within the company.

- Make sure you build a resume in the industry that you would like to work. It should contain vital skills and experiences that will eventually land you that 1st position in the work place. Build your resume with internships and part time jobs.

- My advice is to spend time getting to know professors and others that take an interest in you as an athlete. Many opportunities and conversations open to student-athletes, which regular students do not have access to, and very few take full advantage of them and their possibilities.

- Tap into your alumni, parents, family friends, teachers, coaches, etc. for ideas and leads into post-college employment ideas. Talk-talk-talk and ask lots of questions of these people. You may not realize it, but you have a decent "network" already established through your athletic and personal connections. Many times it's difficult for employers to find good help and the resume-interview process can be time consuming and a headache for both parties. You'd be amazed how many opportunities there are within your network of friends/family/alumni/coaches.

- Be confident without being cocky. After all, you are fresh out of college, and while you may have a lot to share with people in the company, you also have a lot to learn.

- Be able to work within the organization. Utilize the skills that got you there...You were able to network and market yourself as an athlete to get into college, now you need to do the same as you exit. Being able to network and work your way through the organization can help you to move onward and upward.

- Ethics, collegiality, and endurance– life is a marathon, not a sprint, so don't spoil your reputation early: it can only help you as it grows, if tended to wisely.

- Having thick skin, you need to be able to weather the storm in the real world. With sports, things are not always going to go your way, similar to the real world. Stay calm and play your game.

- The sooner you recognize your own weaknesses the sooner your competition will stop beating you because of them. This is an endless cycle and something I learned from sports. You might call this "brutal self assessment". Be your own worst and first critic. This also helps deflect the BS criticism you can get from lousy coaches or lousy bosses.

What Real World Advice Do You Have On Finding A Career?

"What's really important (real world advice, good or bad) in finding, creating and flourishing in a career?"

- Find something you enjoy doing… if you don't enjoy coming to work every day, then there is no way that you will be successful. Do something you like doing. If you like your job, working hard and sacrificing with long hours is a lot easier.

☐ Time management and organization are the backbone of success. Having time to do things you enjoy like family, leisure, and hobbies, only comes when you have the time and the resources to enjoy them.

☐ Figure out what is most important to you. Do you want to solve problems? Be a consultant. Do you want a set routine that you can prepare for? Teach. Do you like constant action? Work on the trading floor at a bank. Do what you are interested in and it will be much easier to succeed.

☐ Real world advice cannot be beat. You need to take summer internships to see what the real world is like. Like any sport, you practice hard for the games, but in the real world it's hard to get another chance.

☐ Find your passion. Maybe your job isn't the best, but the people you work with are super cool and the pay isn't so bad. Or maybe you love your job, but the people you work with are duds but you get enough self fulfillment out of it. Whatever you do, if you don't have a passion, find one. Chances are that will lead you to a similar career where you really enjoy it. I've seen too many people in dead-end jobs and all they do is complain about it. Shut up and do something about it then. No one has just one career anymore like our parents or grandparents did. Welcome to the 21st Century!

☐ I have seven pieces of advice I've picked up along the way:

1. Get a mentor early, but choose wisely.

2. Even if you are really good at office politics, avoid them.

3. Save money so you don't find yourself staying in a job just to pay the mortgage.

4. Don't get an MBA until you have worked for at least three years.

5. Don't get a law degree unless you love the law more than money.

6. Prioritize your ethics, it will keep you in much better company.

7. When people say they love their job, in most cases it is because they love the people they work with. In other words, even lifeguarding will suck if the Captain is a pinhead.

☐ A common theme I keep revisiting is one's personal network. Relationships throughout your life have an uncanny way of coming full circle and that can be a great advantage and/or impediment.

☐ I think the main thing is to try to find something that you really, really have a passion for. If you have an idea about something that you really want to do, get out there and go for it. It's the same as becoming a good player, you have an idea about being at a certain level, and then you go out and earn it. Here's my go-to advice:

1. Take on the crappy projects that have high impact to the company.

2. When you're in a new/unique situation act like you've been there before.

3. Make your boss successful.

4. Find something that you love. One of the reasons you are successful as an athlete is because you love your sport and are willing to work hard for that love. It's the same thing with a career. If you love it, you'll work hard and be successful.

- [ ] The hard work you put forth in your sport will pay off in the professional world. It's about creating habits that will be with you for a long time.

- [ ] I think that being genuinely interested in and passionate about what you do is the most important thing in finding, creating and flourishing in a career. If you're not passionate about it, it's going to be extremely difficult--if not impossible--to do your best work and get maximum enjoyment and fulfillment out of your career. If you find a profession that you love, you will never work a day in your life.

- [ ] Don't compromise on your boss. Sometimes you have to be the one to make an adjustment, but life is short and if you are working for someone you don't respect, who doesn't share your values or whose objectives are not right....they will ultimately take you down with them. You might have to be patient, but putting a lot of effort into finding the right sort of person to work for pays dividends in ways you can't imagine.

- [ ] Stay flexible. No job, nor career, that is worthwhile, is a stagnant monolith of skills and requirements. You have to make sure that you are constantly updating your abilities, learning new techniques and skills, and teaching yourself how to apply these things to your profession in ways that gives you the edge in the business world. Had you told people at Disney animation three decades ago that computer imaging, server processing, computer programming and graphic layout would be a fundamental part of their job today, it would have seemed foolish. Yet the director of Finding Nemo probably had a lot of knowledge in all of those areas. Get an education that lays a foundation for numerous skill sets in the future. You never know what will be required of you in your career, so best to stay as fluid as possible.

- [ ] The 30-year career with one company is a rare thing indeed these days. Flexibility, adaptability, willingness to change/evolve, a willingness to move along with the old standbys of loyalty, reliability and consistency are all cornerstones of a successful career. Your athletic experiences will serve you well towards meeting those demands. Be social; connect with superiors/fellow workers and NETWORK.

- [ ] Be honest. Never lie, cheat or steal. Don't whine, complain or make excuses. Be true to yourself. Most importantly, learn from your mistakes.

- [ ] Lastly, the most important, or one of the most, decisions you can make in your life is who you choose to spend your time with as it relates to friends, family, mentors, coaches, teachers, etc. That decision alone has a tremendous impact on the way an individual thinks, acts, what they place value on, what they become concerned with and the way they move in their life. It is very subtle, but after 5, 10, 20+ years, the impact is profound.

What Specific Skills Did You Acquire As A Competitive Athlete That Helps You In Your Career?

"Can you list specific skills that were learned from competitive athletics that directly enhance (and how they enhance) your career, even today? What additional message(s) would you like to express to men and women competitive athletes today as it applies to 'life after sports' (traps, tricks, wisdom, discipline, expectations, etc.)?"

- Expect a tough few months once your athletic career ends--it's difficult to find a new identity. Once you do, don't be too hard on yourself--it takes time to learn the rules of the new business game, and for muscle memory to be learned so that you're hitting shots (successful business shots) repeatedly.

- Although it has become a bit of a platitude, hard work is often undervalued. Having been an athlete, I am able to draw upon experiences of exceptional physical discomfort (six hours training rides in the rain come to mind), whenever a particular activity seems difficult, these memories quickly contextualize the apparent difficulty.

- I am accustomed to working side-by-side with executives and with clients and am not intimidated by either because I have been in front of coaches, fans, the media, and teammates all through my playing career. Knowing how to communicate with different types of people and being tactful is really important, especially in challenging situations.

- Don't forget that while you were in college, you were able to balance being a great athlete and commit to countless hours of practice and games with the demanding rigors of the classroom and the workload that just being a student entailed. If you managed those two things, you can certainly be a great professional, as you'll need those skills to prioritize your time and basically schedule everything once those demands are put upon you by your new boss. Think of your "life after sports" self not as a student-athlete anymore but as a person-professional. You will need to balance your work with your own life and make sure there's a good balance so you're happy with both.

- Remember that the majority of sports end after college… enjoy it but don't make it your entire life… take the good from it and use it prepare your next step in life (the work world). I knew too many people who spent 2-3 years after their senior season ended, lost and not prepared to take the next step. Don't waste those years… enjoy them… life is still fun after college (and if you have a job, you will have money to do more things!)

- Get comfortable enough in your own skin so that you don't mind making others greater than you ever were or could have been. You can practice this lesson in your first job.

- Don't get out of shape. Physical stamina plays a bigger role in business that you can ever imagine.

- Always volunteer to run your company's Intern program. If you do this consistently and treat these people well, you will find yourself with a global network very quickly.

- Start planning for your future now. Athletics is the greatest gift but few of us are accorded the luxury of using it to support ourselves. You will always have your stories, glorious victories, and agonizing losses to look back upon for motivation.

- Once your out (meaning not getting paid to play) stay out. don't get sucked back in because you'll find yourself at age 30 with no work experience, and no career just bad knees.

- No one person has the answer to what will make you successful. What we do have, through athletics, is a foundation for giving great effort in the hopes of eventual gain. Keep your eyes open, don't be afraid to make mistakes along the way, and know that life is dynamic and forgiving and you have a lot of people who want you to succeed behind you.

- Winning is something that is an opportunity in almost any endeavor. And you do get the same rush from winning in a non-sports environment as you do from a sports contest. Trust that and apply yourself to a non-sports endeavor just as you would to a sports situation. You most likely will find it to be just as fulfilling as becoming a successful athlete. But remember all the hard work you had to put in to become the athlete you are… that same work ethic will need to be there off the field as shortcuts in almost any aspect of life rarely exist.

- What is "Life after Sports"? If sports are and always have been part of your life, why would you ever abandon the rewards they provide? Keep playing, training, recreating, participating throughout your career, your family life, your business trips, vacations, forever. The sporting experience(s) will provide; friendships, balance, health benefits/quality of life and at the very least, a good endorphin high now and then.

- Life after sports is still life. :-) I guess what I really mean is that I think everyone has to figure out why he or she is going to live, and I think most people will find that the reasons they chose to live (consciously or not) while they competed are similar to reasons they find to live once they're done competing. Whoa, that sounds a little too "out there." Sorry!

- Ego is a two-edged sword. As with sports, to achieve success in business you need to be assertive and have confidence. However, too much ego creates arrogance and isolation, traits that do not work well in a collaborative business environment. Sometimes you have to tone down your competitive drive. It can be easy enough to reach the top of the ladder with your experiences and successes in life without running over your competition.

- I was a shy freshman, intimidated by my coaches, Big East basketball, and by my older teammates and it affected my performance on the court and in the classroom. Once I was able to secure the "I was recruited for a reason, I deserve to be here" type of attitude and instill a little confidence in myself, my coaches and teammates began to as well and my performance started to reflect that positive attitude. I ended up a starter and team captain with dean's list grades. It always starts at home, with you. If you don't believe in yourself, why should anyone else? You have to know that before hard work, before determination, it starts with the belief that it can be done.

- [ ] I think the most important thing I have learned, especially from looking back over my playing career and now at my years since college is that confidence is key. Be confident in who you are, in your abilities, and what you feel you can offer the world. If you are confident in yourself, you can achieve anything you put your mind to and that goes for sports, school, and work.

- [ ] "If you can't get in the front door, use the back door". My American Cultural History professor at UCSB told me this when I was a senior and applying for law schools. What he meant was that if I didn't get into the schools I was hoping for, to find a good school and to go for it, e.g., don't give up, keep at it, persevere, be creative, adapt.

- [ ] Preparation is the key to being lucky. But you also need; 1. Leadership skills----they are the same whether on the basketball court, on a project team or running a business; 2. Teamwork skills---the lessons of team play in sports are almost directly transferable to group work efforts; 3. Focus and concentration---the ability to solve the problem at hand rather than failing at that task and 4. Confidence---projecting the air of someone who knows they CAN versus someone who wonders if they can.

- [ ] Tiger Woods uses a golf coach. We all need coaches, mentors, etc. In order to obligate a coach, mentor, friend, teacher into helping you, something must be given in return or exchanged. In some cases it is paying someone for their help, but in other cases money is neither sufficient nor accepted. Being respectful, thankful, gracious, thoughtful, appreciative, and humble is what is required for someone to spend time with you.

- [ ] Don't be afraid to step out of your "athletic self" and experience life after sports. It can be just as challenging and enjoyable as the sport you excelled in. At first it can be difficult and uncomfortable since it's not in your "comfort zone," but in time it will feel more comfortable… just like making a change to your form/stroke/stride/pitch/etc. in your sport. Also, don't be afraid to try something else if your first job isn't to your liking. If you ask 100 ex-athletes, I'd estimate that 95+ would say they are not working the same job or type of job that they started after moving on from their sports careers. Lastly, you don't have to fully give up athletics to pursue a career in the working world. There are numerous opportunities to stay active and even competitive, and to try different activities/sports, which can also be used to expand your network.

Chapter 12

Think Big... but Think Smart

"Remember, today is the tomorrow you worried about yesterday."

⚾ *Most of Us Will Not be Bill Gates or LeBron James*

The best career advice you can be given today is not to be high on motivation, but low on knowledge and skills. Thinking big is no substitute for doing the work, and being smart about your options and decisions is now a requirement.

> *Certainly, you've heard the saying "timing is everything." When it comes to successful athletes making the leap from sports to the workplace, timing is critical. A transitioning athlete has been conditioned to achieve many different goals and objectives throughout their lifetimes, but getting an early jump on career exploration and conducting a successful job search is not an easy task. While every athlete has some sort of eye on what's next, by-and-large, their timing sucks.*

Because most of an athlete's free time is consumed with training or competing, competitive athletes usually start the job search process too late in life. For the same reasons, they are late in understanding what the key components are to finding a job, or they make the wrong assessment of how valuable their athletic careers will be when it comes time to open doors and compete in the workplace. Another problem many athletes face is the cost of missed-opportunity. They miss out on what they could have been doing to explore potential opportunities or people they could have been meeting while they progressed through collegiate and professional sports.

Many athletes are lucky to have a specific guiding path in mind when they begin searching for a job and career exploration; but most do not. The majority of athletes fall into one of two categories:

1. They may not know much about a certain job/career, but something about it sounds interesting. In this case, the athlete has identified a possible career path but hasn't carefully matched it with their personal preferences; or

2. They may have ideas about what they like, but don't know which jobs/careers interest them. In this case, the athlete has identified personal preferences but hasn't matched them with a career path.

Many times, finding a job simply means being the right person at the right time with the right attitude, the right skills, and the right contacts. We've learned that it's not only what you know but who you know that leads to many valuable employment opportunities. As a result, many athletes fall into a job and then evolve into their careers without as much as an ounce of planning and forethought about what they like or dislike. Largely, these important decisions are motivated by happen-chance or short-term financial considerations rather than the long-term goal of true career happiness and a fulfilling work environment.

The sole objective of a successful transition plan for any highly competitive athlete should be to establish a good job/career fit with their interests. It is as much in your interest to be employed in a role for which you are well-suited as it is for the employer to have the right person in the right job. Once you assess your strengths (such as the skills you most enjoy using, the interests that are critical to your sense of job satisfaction, and the values that motivate you to achieve success), you are then ready to explore employment opportunities that best fit your job and career objectives.

Everything is Changing

If you are in college today, aside from athletics, you've spent approximately the last seventeen years sitting in a classroom absorbing bits of knowledge. Every now and then, you were tested to see how well you remembered that information. Occasionally, you had to write a research paper; sometimes quite an extensive one. You were likely given the assignment, and the paper wasn't due for three or four months.

Fast forward to graduation, and suddenly you are out of the safe-haven of the classroom where you were tested on schedule and deadlines were months away. Soon you will be thrust into the harsh reality of your first job. Deadlines will be "Tomorrow at the latest." There are no formal exams, but you get the sense that you are being tested every day. The results come not in report cards, but in performance reviews. Sports? Sorry! Your eligibility is over, or you have been cut from the professional ranks. The enjoyment of a daily workout and practice and the hunt for a championship competing against other schools is now largely reserved for the recreation leagues.

In today's job market, you will need to take increased responsibility for your employment future, upgrade your learning skills, and behave like entrepreneurs. The old days when you are expected to be a loyal employee who could put your long-term employment fate in the hands of a single employer have been eliminated in this new era of multiple jobs, economic resets, down-sizing, and outsourcing. The job you get today may very well disappear in the near future, and the employer you work for today or tomorrow most likely will not be the same one you will be with five years from now. The facts are that most people entering today's job market can expect to undergo three to five career changes and hold more than fifteen different jobs. Long-term loyalty to a single employer is no longer expected, since many people change jobs and employers within a few years.

> *In the world of career preparation, the window is getting narrower, the upside is getting lower, and room for maneuvering is getting scarce. To identify and succeed in finding a great job and satisfying career, nothing in the world can take the place of persistence. Talent will not take the place of persistence... nothing is more common than unsuccessful people with talent. Genius will not take the place of persistence... unrewarded genius is almost a proverb. Education will not take the place of persistence... the world is full of educated derelicts. Persistence and determination alone are the most important factors in a successful career.*

If a highly competitive athlete has acquired one skill as a result of their long sports experience, it's persistence. You are a special breed of individual that is very well-suited for the ever-changing landscape of today's job market, and if you play the game of *CareerBall* well, you will be favored to become tomorrow's leaders. I contend that where once the nerds and academics ruled the business world, the smart athletes will rise to the top because of their unique mix of brains and the abilities they developed through sports– the ability to persevere and to accept or rebound from change, your determination, self-motivation, and competitive instincts. In the coming years, competitive athletes will be highly desired and needed by large and small companies across America.

Be Smart About Your Athletic Career

One of the most challenging things about being a college student-athlete is achieving a well-balanced life, given all the demands you face. The smart athlete knows that having a balanced life will actually help you be a better student and athlete, and the key to a balanced life is self-responsibility. You must make sure you do not forget the importance of establishing relationships outside of the athletic department, finding time to do things other than practice and study, and becoming involved in community as well as university activities.

Many people and groups today consider intercollegiate sports more of a commercial enterprise rather than an academic enterprise. The problem is not that university athletic departments take unqualified students just to have them play sports, but rather that they put so much pressure on them that they can't be real students. Disagreements over how much time is too much time for sports in your life are bound to rage, but the more pressing issue is how to tell whether athletes are fully developing as well-rounded individuals in colleges and universities– and, ultimately, if are they becoming prepared for life after sports at an acceptable pace.

> *I have seen many athletes who have not forgotten where they came from, but their actions make me wonder if they know where they're going. You want to be smart about the pitfalls associated with being a highly competitive athlete. While intoxicating, the thrill and benefits of athletics is short-lived. Getting an early jump on creating a balanced life and preparing for your career is now a requirement for smart athletes.*

Be Smart About Your Education

There are many distractions and academic responsibilities for competitive athletes these days. I'm pretty certain that many student-athletes aren't thinking too much about their employment or financial future. I think it is also a safe bet to say that many professional athletes are focused on making rosters instead of preparing for a career after sports. But here is what we know today as facts:

Fact #1

Even among those student-athletes who make professional rosters, the overwhelming majority will only last a few years in their chosen sports. To put it another way, even if you succeed in professional sports as an athlete, you will still spend thirty to forty years pursuing another career!

Fact #2

If you're in high school, you need to graduate. If you're in college, you need to graduate. Unemployment nationally is now over 10% and the rate for people without a high school diploma is above 17%, while only 6% of those with a college degree or higher were out of work.

Smart athletes know the value of an education and will do whatever is necessary to get their degrees. Don't let athletics get in the way of completing your degree at any cost!

Be Smart About Getting a Variety of Experience

> *It's important to realize, however, that there are no shortcuts to an effective job search or fulfilling career. It takes work– and sometimes disappointment and heartache. I have this saying I like to use: "Experience is what you get when you don't get what you want." It's a good phrase to put on your tombstone, because you can't go through life without making a ton of mistakes. I know plenty of athletes who never take a risk and acquire very little experience. These people are destined to achieve only what is brought to them. Other athletes take risks and fail, only to be left with experience but no results to show. But smart athletes will most likely learn from their experiences and try again, usually with more success the second time around.*

There is no time like college to explore new things in a safe environment. Smart athletes know this is a great time to expand their networks and real world experience. If you are liberal arts major, consider a minor in some course work in accounting, business, marketing, finance, economics, or something else that is vocational. If you're in a vocational major, consider a minor or some course work in a topic that might fuel a unique specialty, such as a foreign language. In today's ultra-competitive job market, every edge helps.

Public speaking skills are particularly important at this stage of your life. These are skills you use every single day and the best skills you can develop for a successful job search and career. Public speaking is not just for politicians! It's a skill that transfers to virtually every career path. If you are afraid of public speaking, it's time to simply speak up in class, speak up during student club meetings or team meetings, and get involved in something that you love to talk about.

Have a hobby. Join a club. Sing in a choir. Act in the community theater. In addition to trying out new things in life, these activities can give you a competitive advantage over less-active peers. Also, pretty much any group activity will provide networking, leadership, and learning opportunities that will help you stand out in your job search. Having a little cultural experience won't necessarily help you in a job interview, but there is a certain level of awareness you will be expected to have.

Colleges like to admit sports team captains, student government officers, club presidents, and first-chair violinists. I'm sure it doesn't surprise you to learn that employers like these types as well. What's so important about being a leader? Leaders are who make things happen, period. Every organization– from businesses to nonprofits, politics to coffee shops– need people who say "This is where we need to go, and I'll make sure you get there."

Be Smart in Your Job Search

Looking for a job is no fun, especially for the shy and sensitive who are forced to introduce themselves to strangers, ask for assistance, and encounter inevitable and hard-to-swallow rejections. But smart athletes realize that depending on how you approach the process, it also can be an extremely educational, exciting, and exhilarating experience. If done properly, you'll meet many new and interesting people.

Smart athletes continue networking throughout their lives. By regularly talking to people about your jobs and careers, you will find a treasure trove of great jobs and opportunities. Networking will be your ticket to job and career advancement. Use all those contacts you made during your athletic life to your advantage. Call up or visit past teammates, parents, coaches, and teachers. See if they know of anyone or any companies you could try to contact for a job, and see if you could use them as a contact. Yes, this is networking. Don't be shy! It's time to ask everyone and anyone if they can point you in a direction for that job lead and start within your career!

> *Smart athletes think like an entrepreneur. You are responsible for your own employment fate. No one owes you a job. Smart athletes find a good mentor or career coach. Attach yourself to someone who you can trust and use to help you sort our opportunities, make decisions, and get your career on track. Smart athletes keep a positive attitude– and that is everything when it comes to getting ahead. Try to keep a positive attitude to everything you say and do. What you will learn repeatedly is that people like working with and promoting enthusiastic and positive people.*

Get your resume looking sharp and prepare some cover letters. Talk to your career center counselors, as many will have connections with local employers looking for graduates from your school. Also, carve out some time in each day to practice cold-calling. This is not as bad as it sounds. Just investigate companies that you think you'd like to work for and why. Write down why you might want to work there and why you think you might be a good fit for that company. Find out from the company website who you should talk to, and send in your letter explaining the above reasons, asking for a meeting to discuss any possibilities or for advice. While not everyone can offer you a job, many people love to talk about their work, so approach it as advice rather than a job.

> *Here is a list of several job search mistakes that have knocked out otherwise great people from the competition. You will want to avoid these mistakes at all costs:*

- ✓ Lack clear goals and work objective
- ✓ Harbor negative and self-defeating can't-do attitudes
- ✓ Misunderstand the sequential nature of the job search
- ✓ Show indications of several ineffective job search activities
- ✓ Failure to network, or network with the wrong people
- ✓ Provide little evidence of skills, commitment, and a productive pattern of behavior
- ✓ Write and distribute poorly written resumes and letters
- ✓ Include negative or incomplete information on applications
- ✓ Commit several job interview sins, from arriving late to failing to close interviews properly
- ✓ Fail to ask questions, listen, and change interview directions if necessary
- ✓ Lack tactfulness and honesty
- ✓ Conducting outdated job search strategies
- ✓ Over relying on technology, especially the Internet
- ✓ Avoid taking risks
- ✓ Unprepared to handle rejections
- ✓ Failed to develop or never prepared a plan of action
- ✓ Exhibit week follow up skills
- ✓ Try to conduct a job search on their own rather than seek professional help at critical steps in the job search

- ✓ Resist changing of poor behaviors and acquire new habits
- ✓ Fail to keep motivated and focused throughout the job search.

Taken together, these mistakes will project an unflattering image of you or paint you as someone who is not quite up to doing the job. Smart athletes keep these negatives from their job search and focus on the positive skills that will always define you as a great hire.

Be Smart About Money

Here's the simple truth: money (income) is simply about bartering. Remember when you take a job that you are basically making a trade-off... "I agree to be paid this amount for this job I am willing to do", period. Yet, many people apply meaning to money that it was never meant to have– such as equating it with love or self-worth or determining how important your job might be. The power of money ruins friendships and frequently destroys marriages and important relationships like roommates, friends, relatives and employers. Smart athletes take the time to understand and raise their money consciousness and begin to exercise better money judgment.

Our childhood messages about money continue to shape our adult lives. These early messages become sacred myths and lead people to repeat the same bad decisions, often ignoring basic financial principles. It's hard to realize (much less understand) the roots of our money consciousness. Some of us are spenders, some of us are cheap, some come from rich, and some from poor backgrounds, and some of us were first exposed to discussions about money when we were eleven years old and our parents were fighting and in the process of getting divorced. Money oftentimes provokes other issues in us– personal issues that you better understand if you are to be successful in your financial future.

> *The hardest lesson to learn for athletes or non-athletes alike is that you need to focus more on maintaining wealth rather than increasing wealth. Sometimes, though, an athlete just can't shake the temptation to try to hit the jackpot. There is something in an athlete's DNA that drives us to swing for the fences financially, and usually at great peril.*

The bottom line is that all athletes need guidance on financial issues, but probably the biggest readjustment most student-athletes need to make is in their own expectations of the real world. For instance, how much money do you think your first job will pay? Studies show that the average student-athlete expects to make $64,500 a year right out of college. For those with a liberal arts or general studies degree, the actual figure is closer to $32,000. Ouch! And to top it off, I don't even know how much that number will decline by way of the recent economic reset that the world wide economy continues to endure.

Whatever the economic environment we live in, you will need to wake up earlier to the financial realities of the world. The good news is that it's not any different for any other member of society and, in fact, it is likely athletes will have the upper hand on the rest of the population when it comes to earning potential and wealth accumulation… if you play it smart.

Be Smart About Your Credit History

The earlier you start educating yourself and planning your financial future, the better off you'll be later in life. It's also important for you to learn how credit affects your life. You really need to be smart and protect your credit because it impacts your ability to do things, to borrow money, and to acquire those things that everyone needs– a credit card, a car, an apartment, a house, a loan and a job.

The days of banks offering you easy, free credit cards are long gone. Through all the foreclosures, staggering stock market losses and declining personal fortunes, banks and lenders will continue to shore up risks well into this decade. They are closing a record amount of credit card accounts and reducing millions of dollars in credit lines. As they clamp down, even some consumers with excellent credit and spotless payment records are seeing credit scores reduced because of diminished credit lines.

Now, when it's already difficult to qualify for loans and credit cards, it will become very difficult to keep your credit scores from falling. Your employment future and even your auto insurance costs can be affected if you don't have a good credit rating; 42% of US employers routinely do credit checks on job applicants, and most auto insurers now take credit scores into account in determining their rates.

If you're just starting out in life (as I suspect you are), it's important to understand that because credit cards are more common than mortgages, your card related decisions are important. Failure to pay a monthly balance on your credit card can hurt overall credit scores more than failure to pay your mortgage! If you have a student loan in your name, chances are your payment record is reported to one of the three national credit reporting agencies. Miss a payment and you might see your credit score slashed resulting in increased rates and possibly a failed job opportunity. Miss a payment and it stays on your credit report for up to ten years.

Smart athletes should have a copy of their credit report and get an idea what type of information the three main credit reporting agencies track. You can view and print your individual credit reports at no-charge (free!) by logging onto www.AnnualCreditReport.com. Pay close attention to the accuracy of all the information reported (name, address, birthdates, cards you may have opened, etc.). This is an excellent means of seeing exactly what goes on in the credit reporting world (and checking for any fraud that might exist on your profile)– something you will have to deal with for the rest of your lifetime.

Be Smart About Lifelong Learning

Since we live in a constantly changing economy and job market, smart athletes are well advised to continue acquiring more skills and keep yourself in the job market on ongoing basis. Today's economy is tough, and whether you work for a company or are an entrepreneur, success is becoming more and more elusive.

I am a huge believer in lifelong education. In my mind, a day in which you have not learned at least one new thing is a wasted day. I also believe that lifelong learning is no longer discretionary but essential for people to bolster their credentials in a volatile marketplace.

Few external forces are going to persuade you to learn once you get out of school. The desire has to come from within. Once you decide you want to make lifelong learning a habit, it is up to you to make it a priority in your life. It's like exercise or the development of your athletic fundamentals in that if it's not a priority, you are likely to not do it.

Lifelong learning is one of the keys to becoming an outstanding performer in your life and in your career. Smart athletes know that if you make learning a priority in your life, you will be successful at whatever you pursue.

🏐 Be Smart About "Plan B"

Commit to Plan A, but always have a Plan B. Turbulent times often become difficult times for people who fail to anticipate and adjust to new changes. Athletes who do not have interests outside of their sport often have difficulty adjusting to life once their formal sports career ends.

> *If you put 100% of your energy into your sport, you may be vulnerable to problems if anything planned or unplanned restricts you from participating in that activity. The smart athletes who adjust most easily are those who have achieved their sport goals and at the same time had an alternative focus for their energies. During college, these individuals may have had sports as a primary discipline, but they also had other activities or academic pursuits as their secondary interests. Once they graduate, they shift sports into a secondary role and focus primarily on their secondary interests.*

Even if you are presently an elite or professional athlete or still hope to play professionally after college, you may find it helpful to develop a contingency plan– an alternative plan to develop in case your main plan does not work. This is your Plan B. Contingency plans are very helpful for athletes, because career ending injuries and being passed over in the selection process are always possible. Even if you are able to have professional career, you will probably need to pursue another career later in life, and having an alternative focus is just plain smart.

The saying "Failure to plan is planning for failure" is very applicable in career development. If you fail to adequately plan, you will struggle to keep your head above water if something doesn't go your way. To be effective, you must always have a Plan B up your sleeve. "What if I can't get a job in this crappy economy?...What if I get fired or laid off?" Trying to anticipate what can go wrong and having backup in case it does will prevent a lot of heartache and stress.

Graduate School? A Pretty Good Option

> *For any athlete who wants to rise to the top of their chosen post-sports profession, I like the idea of a post-graduate degree. Advanced degrees are becoming another means for employers and hiring managers to systematically choose one candidate over another. Typically, possessing an advanced degree opens the doors to tight labor markets, quicker advancement, higher earning potential, and more career choices. Also, in a poor economy, going back to school might just be a safe place to be, assuming you can adequately afford the costs and loans required while you are not partaking of full-time employment.*

The graduate degree of choice for most collegiate athletes is the Master's of Business Administration (MBA). If you are planning on pursuing your MBA or another graduate-level degree, it is important to be aware of the special challenges surrounding your choice. Here are four factors shaping MBAs today.

1. Competition for slots will be fierce

Are you up for a challenge? Classes won't become super-sized to accommodate the application surge, so admissions will be ultra-competitive, and fewer applicants will get in. The Graduate Management Admissions Council (GMAC) reports that 263,979 GMAT exams were administered worldwide in 2010, very close to the all-time record of 264,700 set in 2009. The number of GMAT exams taken by women hit a record 105,900 during testing year 2010, an increase of 36% during the past five years and the first time female test takers have exceeded 100,000 in a single testing year. A total of 30,264 GMAT exams were taken by Chinese citizens in 2010 and although still far behind the world-leading 127,061 tests taken by US citizens, the 2010 testing level for Chinese citizens represents a substantial rise from the 23,550 last year and nearly a 200% increase from the 10,142 in 2006. Net: competition is increasing.

If getting in has become harder across the board, students will likely apply to more schools to increase their chances. With a fatter stack of applications to choose from, middle-tier schools could shock prospective students with rejection letters they didn't expect.

2. Loans for international students are evaporating

With the credit crunch, student loan programs are disappearing overnight. Citibank has cancelled its CitiAssist loan program, which has left many international students high and dry unless they have lived in the US or have a cosigner who is a US citizen.

Additionally, if they do manage to get into school to get that MBA degree, a weak market means international students will have to really stand out among job applicants if they hope to obtain the elusive H1-B visa. With the deck stacked against them in the United States, more students will apply to B-schools in their own countries.

3. Quitting a job is risky

Putting aside a lucrative career to attend business school has always given potential students pause, especially during an economic slump. Traditionally, students who postpone or quit jobs at the start of a recession graduate with an MBA when the economy is in an upswing. But no one is able to predict with certainty how long a recession or economic downturn will last.

In the past, predictors of the "opportunity cost" of going to business school in a downturn have been skewed by the apparent end of big salaries and juicy bonuses in investment banking. Those monster salaries on Wall Street have all but vanished, except for only the best and the brightest. Still, opportunities could be missed if you forego earning your advanced degree. Remember what we learned about self-responsibility... Not making an investment in yourself can turn around and haunt you when the economy goes back up. If you are weighing the pros and cons of graduate school, it would be wise to educate yourself on the requirements of your industry or chosen career path before you make the decision to go for that post-graduate degree.

4. The learning is still valuable

As today's business schools create case studies based on the Wall Street debacle and the crash of the worldwide banking and automotive industries, no one doubts that what you learn in your studies for an MBA will be extremely valuable when the economy steadies.

Students may need to adjust their career goals and possibly their salary expectations, though. The bottom line? This is a good time to park yourself in an MBA program and build up your portfolio of intellectual capital. Graduates will emerge in two years or so and be in a much different market, and you'll be glad you took the advice of this section.

Are Certificate Programs the Way to Go?

In a tough economy, going back to school can be financially unrealistic, but short-term certificates can meet many of the same needs without breaking the bank. And while they might not have much in the way of glamour, a six or nine-month course can do wonders for a career.

Many colleges and universities offer dozens of certificate programs, and there are classes for just about any field of interest. The top four choices are currently in:

- Finance,
- Human resources,
- Healthcare, and
- Project management.

While there have been a lot of layoffs within the financial services sector, all indications are that there will be an increased need for people who know about money and the financial system. This is especially true with the Baby Boomers hitting retirement and needing to know how to preserve what is left of their savings.

Creative types can also find a slew of certificate programs that match their interests. Some of the more common choices are programs that provide exposure to newer technologies, such as graphic design or mechanical drawing. A certificate in the music recording industry has also seen a rise in popularity, which is attributed to the simple mathematics of more affordable technology. These days, pretty much anyone can set up a music studio for a few thousand dollars and produce sound that is the same quality as Beatles recordings. Ten years ago, it took $100,000 or more to make a short film. Now the biggest expense associated with a short film is feeding the cast and crew on the set, while the technology is a fraction of what it once cost.

One of the major reasons why people enroll in certificate programs is to earn a higher salary... and it often works. Legal assistants and professionals who work as certified legal assistants or certified paralegals earn thousands of dollars more per year than those who perform the same duties but are not certified. An investment of a few thousand dollars in a certificate program can result in tens of thousands of dollars in increased earnings over the course of a career.

> *As for those just starting out on their careers, many experts are giving three letters of advice: CPA. The occupation of Certified Public Accountant has become the most valuable certificate coming out of college, not to mention the least risky. It goes on your resume forever, you can utilize the experience to make better financial decisions in your own life, and you don't have to practice accounting your whole career to reap the benefits of a CPA.*

While there are obvious benefits, there are still a few problems with certificate programs. One problem that can befall students is confusion about how to actually obtain the certificate. Often, you cannot earn your certificate simply by completing the certificate program at your school In many cases, there is a professional group that issues licenses and official certifications, usually with a nationally administered examination. Some career paths (CPA license, for example) require work experience in addition to the exam and the completion of courses.

The bottom line is: people are changing jobs and advancing careers in ways they never have before. Certification gives people a transition into a higher level in their career and sometimes into completely different field... but if this is a path you pursue, be sure you are clear on all that you need to do to obtain your certification and license.

Be Smart About Your Generation

Imagine the impact of millions of your teammates and friends transitioning from college, sports, and into the economy. Your generation is filled with fresh-thinking, energized kids, armed with the most powerful human capital in history, hitting the workforce all at once. This wave has just begun. You are part of the Millennial Generation (Millennials) and there are about 80 million of you born between 1980 and 1998. You will transform the nature of the enterprise and how wealth is created as your culture will become the new culture of work, rapidly taking over from the baby boomers who are now pushing 60.

> *Your generation is exceptionally curious, self-reliant, contrarian, smart, focused, able to adapt, high in self-esteem, and globally-oriented. Unlike your parents, you and other young people in this generation thrive on collaboration and abhor the notion of a boss. Your first point of reference is the Internet. You strive to innovate and require fast results. You love hard work because work, learning, and play coincide. You are creative in unimaginable ways. A bigger proportion of your contemporaries than of any other generation will seek to be entrepreneurs. Smart organizations can learn from you.*

As a smart athlete, you are uniquely qualified to lead your generation and shape the new structure of work and career. **When opportunity knocks, answer the door**!

Chapter 13

Current Employment Trends Shaping the New Economy

While many individuals look towards the future with unshakeable optimism, there's good reason to be less than optimistic than ever before. Economically speaking, the decade ahead may well be the worst of times for many people, but if you take the time to spot trends and react accordingly, not everyone will be without a job or a career.

Athletes have some experience with scouting the competition and adjusting game plans to ensure a favorable result– you are programmed to WIN! Beginning your career plans early enough in the game and making progress towards positioning yourself within a growing industry and region are some of the very first steps successful job-hunters take to win in the job market.

The concept of a career is deeply rooted in the post-World War II era of big corporations. Until the 1990s, many individuals pursued careers, often within a single organizational setting. Given the changing structure of the job market, the decline of traditional career paths, and increased interest in pursuing satisfying lifestyles, the future will witness the gradual erosion of careers.

More and more individuals today and in the decade ahead will be interested in finding specific jobs which may, or may not be related to careers. The need for a paycheck in a world scarce of income opportunities is dictating this sort of temporary appeasement.

> *However, there may be a distinct advantage for the athlete in this sort of competitive environment where the jobs are scarce and the applicants are many. Many employers are taking a new look at highly competitive individuals that can stare down dire times, bring optimism and a work ethic to the party, and continue to build for the future. If the choice is between hiring an individual that has zero experience in difficult, challenging environments that call on resourcefulness and competitive instincts or someone who possesses a lifetime of these important skills and knows how to effectively present them, the choice becomes clear. They will choose the one who can keep his or her head in the game and keep pushing for the win.*

A lot of students and athletes accustomed to achieving exactly what they seek want that perfect needle-in-the-haystack job, but in the new economy, that's just not entirely possible. Conventional wisdom says that the most important thing for the new college graduate to do is to keep busy. Ideally, students don't want to have an empty void on the resume after graduation, but the prospect of working for free at a nonprofit or flipping burgers with a college degree does not sit well with students who need cash to live on and repay their student loans.

Many students are planning to stall the inevitable job hunt by going to graduate school, knowing that the statistics are definitely better for employment if you possess a graduate degree. But prolonging graduation by a year or two may put them in the same situation they are currently in… and if you're an athlete that already possesses very little work experience, the prospect of a two-year delay before entering the workforce may not be worth the wait.

Career Trends to Watch in The New Economy

If you were to scan the headlines of the business pages of any major newspaper, you might wonder about your chances of getting the job. Readers are bombarded every day with negative economic forecast and announcements of major corporate layoffs. The truth is that people are still finding jobs. Employment is shifting away from large corporations towards smaller, emerging companies. The shift seems to be fueled by several recent corporate trends.

- *Downsizing.* Companies need many fewer workers to perform required tasks due to technology innovation and efficiency.

- *Mergers, takeovers, and acquisitions.* Many corporations are buying out their competitors or merging with similar businesses and are therefore able to eliminate positions.

- *Outsourcing.* Corporations have discovered that it costs less to have outside companies perform some of the tasks that employees once performed.

As these trends shrink the corporate work force, a major upswing has occurred in the number of new companies and consulting firms in the technology and services industries. These smaller companies and firms are expanding rapidly and will continue to offer large number of varied employment opportunities that are ideally-suited for athletes and the athlete DNA.

> *No one can predict the future, but spotting emerging trends is possible. As a result of the recent run-up in the US economy over the past 20 years and the resulting re-correction or economic reset, some natural trends are starting to emerge. It is very important to know about these trends and to assess the importance of each in your career planning and development.*

Smaller companies may offer more job security.

Each week brings news of more and more layoffs at some of America's largest and most influential companies. This may indicate that time is right to move to a more modestly-sized organization. While small companies don't offer any immunity from being laid off, they can be more nimble than large companies, reacting more quickly to business climate turnarounds. Small companies are taking advantage of this time to upgrade their talent, so don't rule out the small guys! Plus, athletes tend to be entrepreneurial in nature and are generally not afraid of risks, so you will see a greater number of former athletes running these small companies.

Be willing to work part-time or on a temporary basis.

Over the last decade, we've been seeing more companies looking to hire people on a part-time, temporary or project basis, and each recession accelerates that interest. Employers today are fighting to control the cost in what has become a service economy, and employee costs are specifically under constant scrutiny. Using contractors and freelancers can keep the company lean during lean times. Companies don't want to go through big layoffs; they are aware of the damages such drastic action can cause, so they're turning more and more to a self-employed workforce. If you have interest in a skill that can be shaped into a one-person shop, don't be afraid to think of yourself as your first employer!

Expect a pause or two in the hiring process.

Even if you're the ideal candidate for a job and the hiring manager is busy checking your references, an offer may not be immediately forthcoming. Hiring freezes won't be uncommon, but even when an organization is staffing up, the process could be lengthy. And there are more candidates out there, so companies will be more careful and look for the best fit. The fact is, most companies are not hiring willy-nilly as they often do in times of expansion. Be patient, but be prepared to say "yes" to almost anything a hiring manager asks of you. Once in the door, you can prove your worth and begin to control those factors that you were unable to at the time of your hire.

People will postpone their retirement.

While this may not affect you (as you are most likely in your entry-to-early career stage), many folks will be working long past even the most well-planned retirement. Between a poorly performing stock market, Ponzi schemes, and a weak real estate market, many people will need to work an extra three to five years past their planned retirement. If you are seeking employment with a company who appears to have a large staff of older workers, it might not be a right fit for you– for there is a reason many of those employees are still working. And remember, youthful energy always has a place within any company, but you may find yourself working with someone your parent's age rather than the hottie you hoped for. So, be respectful of your elders... always.

There will be a big push for infrastructure repair.

You can't go a day without reading about how our nation's infrastructure– bridges, roads, levies, etc.– is falling apart and badly in need of repair. There are multiple rebuilding programs that have been created at the federal and state levels, and this translates to millions of new jobs. The infrastructure and rebuilding program to create jobs will be available to those who aggressively seek to be a part of it. And don't think infrastructure only means construction work... it also means engineering, manufacturing, staffing, management and a host of service jobs for men and women who are willing-minded and able-bodied.

Wall Street is not what it used to be.

If you're thinking of a career on Wall Street, do not be too quick to forget the recent massacre on Wall Street and the economic downturn it created. It was unlike previous downturns, as in 2001, when laid-off traders and investment banks reinvented themselves as hedge fund managers; or in the early 1990s, when laid-off workers were scooped up by foreign banks. Trading floors will continue to shrink even further, and so will the ranks of bankers and the other geniuses who created this most recent downturn. If your parents were successful Wall Street types who made it big for a long period of time, call or text them and congratulate them for being in the right place at the right time. But don't necessarily think it is time to follow in their footsteps because that path has a lot of debris in the way.

It's Young vs. Old in the face-off for jobs.

With unemployment at a twenty-six-year high and many older workers chasing entry-level jobs like those they held a half-century ago, sixty-five has become the new twenty. Millions of older Americans have delayed retirement because of plummeting 401(k)s, soaring healthcare costs, and the realization that Social Security benefits are too little to live on, or all of the above. This delay has made it harder for millions of young workers to climb onto the first rung or two of the career ladder, especially since many employers favor hiring applicants with a track record. It will be your skills, charm, and doing the important things you learn in *CareerBall* that will help you out maneuver your grandparents for that job at Abercrombie & Fitch!

In a bad economy, a premium is placed on those with prior experience.

With the economy the way it is, many employers don't want to hire people they have to train. They want people who are hands-on right away. This is why many businesses prefer older workers; they're dependable and reliable, they show up, and somewhere along the line, they have developed customer service skills. Older workers also take less sick days and are more prone to use sick time in an honest manner instead of calling in ill to spend a day at the beach. One category where young people have advantage is that they possess broad technical skills and are creative problem-solvers. It is well-known that athletes possess a host of valuable soft skills, and those athletes that have carved out time for internships or summer jobs will find their resumes at the top of the heap. Again, this is why you should be thinking about your real life career in the early stages of your athletic career. If you took the time to orchestrate internships and summer jobs when you were younger, you will have an easier time nailing down a job after you finish your sporting career.

Take a second look at jobs within the federal government.

The federal government is continuing to boost campus recruiting ahead of anticipated worker shortages. By 2016, nearly 61% of current full-time government employees will be eligible for retirement. There are 193,000 mission-critical jobs that need to be filled in the next two years, and these are meaningful jobs that assist our country in solving its most pressing problems. The 2,000,000 strong federal workforce, with 85% employed outside the Washington DC area, spans the entire professional range of opportunities– astronomers, zoologists, finance, and even real estate. Every private sector job has a close cousin in the federal workforce, and while this is a wide and varied employer with jobs ranging from the FBI to Homeland Security to the Department of the Interior, qualifications and competition are stiff. Look into the requirements closely, especially if you have some "questionable behavior" that is of public record.

More graduates are entering the workforce than ever before.

In the future, college graduates may have more trouble landing a jobs than their predecessors, as employers continue to trim their hiring outlooks in response to the slowing economy and financial-sector turmoil. Colleges and universities will grant an estimated 1,585,00 Bachelor's degrees this school year, up from 1,544,000 in the prior year. The employment outlook is bad, but it's not all bad. Despite cutbacks in finance, retail, construction, and manufacturing, demand for recent graduates remains high in fields such as accounting, public service, healthcare, education, and technology. According to the Bureau of Labor Statistics, the following jobs will see the most increase throughout the next ten years:

- Network systems, data communications analyst
- Housekeepers and other personal work
- Home health aides
- Computer software engineers, applications
- Veterinarian technologists and technicians
- Personal financial advisors
- Certified public accountants
- Makeup artists, theatrical and performance
- Medical assistance professionals (nursing, physician assistant, x-ray technicians)
- Veterinarians
- Substance abuse, behavioral disorder counselors

14 Emerging Trends You Should Also Keep Your Eye On

> *The future holds great promise for the American worker, and you will have many exciting career opportunities to capitalize upon. In addition to the above-mentioned trends, there are a number of emerging economic and employment indicators that you should be aware of as you plan your career, select your major, or are preparing to move into the workforce for the first time after a career in athletics.*

1. **As baby boomers move into retirement** and the birth rate continues at near-zero population growth rates, fewer young people will be available for entry-level positions in the coming decade. There is also a shortage of competent workers with basic experience and

learning skills, which is creating serious problems in further developing and maintaining a strong US economy. Given the double whammy of nearly 30,000,000 functionally illiterate adults in our country who are unable to read, write, or perform simple computations, combined with a shrinking number of fewer easily trainable, young entry-level workers, a large portion of the workforce jobs will remain unfilled. This is despite the fact that 2,000,000 to 3,000,000 new jobs are created each year. Many of these adults will remain permanently unemployed or under-employed, contributing little to economic growth, while major labor shortages will exist. If you are an athlete who plans on graduating from college, the future will be a very bright place if you exercise patience and plan for the long haul.

2. **While a renewed and strong US manufacturing** sector will create fewer new jobs, face-to-face service industries will be responsible for most job growth in the decade ahead. The American manufacturing industry is becoming one of the strongest economic sectors in terms of production output… but the weakest sector in terms of its contribution to job growth and job creation. Plan accordingly.

3. **Long-term employment security and income** will continue to be tied to high levels of education. During the past few decades, individuals have been well advised to get a college education or continue to pursue an advanced degree. In many of the top technical and scientific fields, statistics have shown most of those employed held, at the very least, a four-year college degree. We now live and operate in a global economy that places highly-educated and skilled workers from low wage countries in direct competition with similar skilled workers in America. In other words, competition is rising not only from the US colleges and universities, but from the entire world. The education level you ultimately achieve will most likely have a distinct employment and economic impact during your lifetime that may very well be tied to your overall career success. Your parents and teachers were right: get a college education! You'll have a safe and secure employment future– a comfortable spot in the new high-tech and service-oriented global economy.

4. **A series of domestic and international incidents** such as shocks like 9/11 and other unique events are becoming more and more commonplace and are likely to continue emerging in the early twenty-first century. In addition to the obvious effects of these events, it also creates a ripple of new boom and bust cycles for employment. The list of possible scenarios that will affect employment opportunities seems endless: international crisis in developing third and fourth-world economies, countries with radical movements, the disintegration and developing regions within Eastern Europe, energy and precious metal shortages due to depletion of current stock, regional military conflicts, and the collapse of financial markets. All of these (and more) contribute to an unstable world economic crisis and employment market. Difficulties in the banking, energy, and telecommunications markets are still a very real part of the American landscape. We are also in the midst of water shortages in the Southwest, environmental issues such as global warming and acid rain, and major health issues and potential international pandemics such as HIV, AIDS and the avian and swine flus. These will inevitably create a chain reaction of new crisis and threaten millions of people worldwide. And we haven't even mentioned earthquakes, hurricanes, and tornadoes that create economic shocks to regional economies, as well as affect the overall national economy. Jobs will be created and lost faster than ever in such an unstable world.

5. **There are also major shortages of skilled crafts people** that will create numerous production, distribution, and service problems in the coming decade. The fact is that fewer individuals receive training in blue-collar occupations, and interest among the young in blue-collar trades has substantially and noticeably declined. The impact of these changes will continue to be felt in the early twenty-first century as production service industries that require highly skilled crafts people and companies that fix things experience serious labor shortages. Repairing your car, your major appliances, and your machines will become very expensive services that were traditionally provided by highly-skilled crafts people who no longer exist in the numbers required to keep up with production.

6. **What we used to call retirement will continue to be postponed.** In the future, more job and career choices will be available for the elderly who are either dissatisfied with traditional retirement or can simply no longer afford the high costs of retirement. Many people will never retire, preferring instead part-time or self-employment in their later years. Others will retire from one job and start new careers even well after age fifty. Social Security benefits continue to decline, and the higher costs of retirement will further transform retirement practices and systems in the decade ahead.

7. **Women will continue to flood the labor market,** dispelling traditional "home with the kids" roles and compete for all kinds of jobs and careers. More will enter non-traditional *occupations* such as engineering, construction, high-tech, and sports, which have been largely the mainstay of men. Women will account for two-thirds of the growth in all occupations over the next ten years.

8. **Part-time and temporary employment opportunities will increase.** Temporary employment services will continue experiencing booming business as more and more companies attempt to cut personnel costs as well as achieve greater personnel flexibility by hiring a large number of temporary employees for whom they do not have to have insurance or benefits. Part-time and contingency workers will constitute a recognized and desirable class of workers. Given economic uncertainties, the high costs of hiring, and the distinct advantages of working with employment firms that manage contingency workers, more and more employers will replace full-time employees with contingency workers. Many businesses employing 100 or fewer employees will rely on contingency workers to make up 30% of their staff.

9. **The need for a smarter workforce** with specific technical skills will continue to impact the traditional education system as both businesses and parents demand greater job and career reality in educational curriculums. Expensive and overly bureaucratic, many traditional four-year colleges and universities will face stable-to-declining full-time enrolment, as well as the flight of quality faculty to more challenging lucrative jobs outside academia.

10. **Union memberships will continue to decline** as more blue-collar manufacturing jobs disappear and interest in unions wanes among both blue and white-collar employees. As union membership declines, union workers continue to find themselves on the defensive, with little choice other than to agree to management demands for greater worker productivity and fewer benefits– especially when it comes to the elimination of costly defined-benefit pensions.

11. **The population will continue to move** into suburban and semi-rural communities as high-tech industries and services move in this direction. Large and older central cities continue to bear disproportionate welfare, tax, and criminal justice burdens through the declining industrial base, deteriorating structures, relatively poor and unskilled populations, and high rates of crime. Urban populations will continue to move into suburban and semi-rural communities developing their own economic base. There were once bedroom communities that served large cities, and now these communities will have their own economic base and will provide employment for the majority of local residents.

12. **An increasing number of skilled and high-tech service jobs** will move offshore. As US businesses take advantage of cheap skilled labor and high-speed communications, many businesses are already exporting their accounting, design, telemarketing, and data management functions to India, the Philippines, and Mexico via the Internet, faxes, and next-day delivery from couriers like DHL and FedEx. If you've called in to any big Customer Service lines as of late, you might have noticed this trend because you might speak to someone working thousands of miles overseas.

13. **The number of small businesses will continue to increase** as new opportunities for entrepreneurs arise in response to the high-tech, Internet, and service revolutions, and as more individuals find new opportunities to experiment with changing careers. Over 900,000 new businesses will be starting each year during the coming decade. This growth in new companies will generate 90% of all new jobs created each year. The number of business failures will increase accordingly, especially during the bust cycles of boom-and-bust economies. Large Fortune 500 companies will further downsize their operations to meet global pressures. It is projected that companies with fewer than five employees will generate most of the new job growth, and some of the best job opportunities will be with growing companies that employ fewer than fifty people.

14. **Here's a trend that's interesting:** the fastest-growing jobs category in the decade ahead will be for people without a four-year degree. A disproportionate number of opportunities will be low-wage, low-skill jobs in service industries. These would include positions such as janitors and custodial workers, day workers, healthcare aides, security guards, and grounds keepers. Most of these jobs will be face-to-face. They cannot be automated or exported offshore. Before you get all fired up about these prospects, bear in mind that while your athletic background probably equipped you with a high school diploma and the basic skills necessary for many of these job opportunities, setting your sights on this type of work may throw you into the growing ranks of the working poor. You don't want that, and I don't want you to experience that life. You can do better, and you should! Set your sights higher, and don't just settle.

🎯 Business-as-Usual is a Thing of the Past

Here are a few other trends that will affect your career:

> *Opportunities for career advancement will become increasingly limited within most organizations. Organizations will have difficulty providing career advancement, especially with the ever-popular flat organizational charts and workers postponing their retirement well into future years. Other factors that will limit future advancement opportunities include:*

- ✓ The growth of small businesses that operate with very limited organizational hierarchies,
- ✓ The continuing focus on non-hierarchical forms of organization,
- ✓ The tendency to hire managers from outside the organization.

Overall job satisfaction in the future will become less geared towards climbing the organizational ladder and more towards job duty satisfaction and organizational benefits. The issue of job satisfaction will become a major problem, as many organizations will experience difficulty in retaining highly qualified personnel. Greater competition, fewer promotions, frustrated expectations, greater discontentment, and job-hopping will be on the rise.

As middle management positions continue to be eliminated as part of overall downsizing efforts, managerial and executive turnover will increase accordingly. The problem will be especially pronounced for many women and minorities, who have traditional aspirations to advance to the top but will be blocked by the flood of managers and executives from the Baby Boomers generation, who are trying to survive at both the middle and top of their organizations.

> *Job-hopping will increase as more and more individuals learn how to change careers. As more job and career options become available for the skilled, savvy worker, as pension systems become more portable, as more people use the Internet to browse job opportunities, as job search and relocation techniques become more widely known, more and more individuals will change jobs and careers in the decade ahead. If ever there was a time to really master the basics of searching for, and getting a job, that time has arrived.*

Benefits packages will undergo increased scrutiny as more and more organizations cut back on personnel expenses. Traditional high-cost health insurance and pension plans will be reassessed by employers and subject to continuous cutbacks. More and more employers will require employees to make significant contributions to health insurance and retirement plans.

Apprenticeship programs will increase in number as the nation attempts to train and retrain a skilled labor pool for high-demand service industries. The coming shortage of skilled labor to service everything from air conditioners to automobiles is directly related to the decline of apprenticeship programs and the lack of interest in pursuing careers in the trades. Individuals not pursuing higher education degrees will find five times the available career opportunities through such programs, as compared to those who compete for traditional white-collar jobs.

Don't Lose Hope... Ever!

For every big company that's downsizing, you have a generic company that's opening a new line and creating production, quality control, operator jobs, and the white-collar support that goes with it. And just because you read about industries shrinking, don't assume there are no opportunities left. For example, the pharmaceutical industry, a long supporter and employer of collegiate athletes, is laying off and hiring at the same time.

If you're adventurous, you can always bet on yourself during these rough times. If there's something you've always wanted to do, now is the time to give it a try. Take a step back and forget about all the baggage and all the doom and gloom. Ask yourself, "What do I really like to do?", and then go out a try to make it happen.

Competition for today's hot jobs will be fierce, but as an athlete, you are no stranger to competition. Jobs are not and will not be as safe as they once were. And even after selecting a career path that seems to have a good prospect for employment, you'll find that getting the job you want in today's economy requires much skill and direct action. People who rely on the once traditional job-hunting method of reading the Help Wanted ads and sending out resumes to every job as close to their area of training and experience will only succeed in receiving many rejection letters.

> *In the near future, I think people are going to be more focused on what do rather than what they earn. As a result, you need to know what you want to do, have a specific game plan to get it, and work hard to give yourself the best chance to get the right job. Remember, you should consider getting a job, a job unto itself. As such, you need to spend ample time, energy, and resources to be successful. But don't worry about your future! It will come together and, like most former athletes, you will be very successful.*

Chapter 14

Need More Help?

Many athletes express frustration and difficulty caused by the forced transition from a lifetime of sports to a meaningful, non-sports-related working environment. Compounding the problem, athletes today are facing a radical change in how the work world is structured and how the economy is shaped. Business-as-usual has been replaced with a rather complex environment of unknowns.

> *Investing in your career is one of the smartest things you can do financially. These days, hiring managers are faced with too many applicants who appear to be equally as qualified as the person who is ultimately hired. Today, you must possess a good grasp of your skill sets, know the value you can bring to an organization, and have the ability to communicate why you would be the best candidate to hire or promote.*

A very important component of career development is career counseling and career coaching. Career counseling is the process of self-exploration combined with looking into and navigating the complex world of work. Life issues are a big part of your work issues, and integrating them both into the counseling process makes for a well-rounded approach to career development.

Make an Appointment With the Career Center!

In addition to the academic advisors in that may be available within the athletic department, were you aware that the on-campus Career Center provides a wide range of Programs and Services for student-athletes? Did you know that they can even serve you in your first year? If you're a freshman, your future academic studies will be based upon the career you want to develop so discussing options when you arrive will provide you a big edge later on in the competitive job market.

Here is a list of the some of the services you can access at the Career Center:

- Individual Career Counseling
- Internships & International Opportunities
- Career Workshops
- Online Jobs & Internships

- Employer Information Sessions
- On-campus Job Interviews
- Job Search or Jump Start Conferences
- Resume Critique
- Career Fairs
- Graduate and Professional School and Study Abroad counseling
- Library, Electronic, and Computer-Based Resources in the Career Lab
- Pre-Professional Career Services
- Letters of Reference Services
- PhD & Master's Career Services
- Networking Opportunities
- Academic & Non-Academic Job Search Tips
- Salary Comparisons, Work Personality Assessments and more!

Don't be like most student-athletes and wait until your eligibility expires. Get into the Career Center today and learn what resources are available to you and get a jump on your competition.

Register with CareerAthletes.com

Once you have made an appointment with the Career Center and reviewed all the terrific services they offer, you will want to register with CareerAthletes.com. For over 12 years, Career Athletes (**www.careerathletes.com**) has been the premium destination for current and alumni student-athletes seeking to create professional connections with mentors and business organizations. Career Athletes possesses the largest member based community of collegiate and elite athletes, representing a growing legion of athletes, athletic departments and hundreds of national, regional and local employers.

Once registered, you will receive an online, Career Athletes Dashboard. This customized, secure site will match your stated preferences and automatically connect you with every new and exclusive job posting from local and national employers, give you access to mentor registrations from your own college athletic and extended alumni family, use of a national search engine of all jobs posted on the Internet, and most importantly, direct contact with employment recruiters who will want to talk to you.

Don't worry: Career Athletes does not charge any fees to any individual user for their online service and is 100% compliant with all NCAA rules and regulations.

Good Luck

Your career, as it has been in sports, will ultimately be measured by the amount effort and discipline you commit to the process. Good luck, and always remember to enjoy the game of *CareerBall*!

About the Author

Russ Hafferkamp

Career Coach and Mentor, NCAA All American and successful CEO

Russ is the Founder and CEO of the Athlete Success Network, Inc. and Managing Director and Co-Founder of Career Athletes, LLC (*www.careerathletes.com*). Russ is recognized as a leader and coach in the career development of collegiate and elite athletes. He has been a speaker at major corporations and leading universities and has been featured in mainstream and sports industry media for his pioneering success in this area. He currently has a private career counseling and coaching practice, providing advice and counsel to over 500 former collegiate and elite athletes as they navigate a successful transition from sports to the working world.

As a business executive with over 20 years experience heading a variety of market-leading technology and consumer-product companies, Russ has managed the human resource development of thousands of sales, service, finance, operations, science, and technical employees for large and start-up companies. As a competitive athlete, Russ has been an NCAA and USA Water Polo All American, has won numerous national and world championships and still competes and coaches for The Olympic Club of San Francisco. He has been a successful NCAA Men's and Women's Head and Assistant Coach at Division I California universities and holds elite coaching certification from USA Water Polo.

Russ currently serves as an advisor and consultant to a number of early stage entrepreneurial organizations and career mentor to many former competitive athletes. He lives in northern California and watches his two daughters, Kelsey and Molly, compete in Water Polo with an ever-present eye on their career planning.

For more information about the author, visit *www.careerball.net.*

Made in the USA
Charleston, SC
01 May 2013